Attention
Deficit
Disorder

Attention Deficit Disorder

by Barbara Sheen

Library of Congress Cataloging-in-Publication Data

Sheen, Barbara.
    Attention deficit disorder/ by Barbara Sheen.
        p. cm. — (Diseases and disorders)
    Includes bibliographical references and index.
        ISBN 1-56006-828-0 (hbk.)
    1. Attention-deficit hyperactivity disorder—Juvenile
literature. 2. Attention-deficit-disordered children—
Juvenile literature. 3. Behavior disorders in children—
Juvenile literature. [1. Attention-deficit hyperactivity
disorder.] I. Title. II. Diseases and disorders series
RJ506.H9 S538 2001
616.85'89—dc21   00-010557

Table of Contents

"The Most Difficult Puzzles Ever Devised"

CHARLES BEST, ONE of the pioneers in the search for a cure for diabetes, once explained what it is about medical research that intrigued him so. "It's not just the gratification of knowing one is helping people," he confided, "although that probably is a more heroic and selfless motivation. Those feelings may enter in, but truly, what I find best is the feeling of going toe to toe with nature, of trying to solve the most difficult puzzles ever devised. The answers are there somewhere, those keys that will solve the puzzle and make the patient well. But how will those keys be found?"

Since the dawn of civilization, nothing has so puzzled people—and often frightened them, as well—as the onset of illness in a body or mind that had seemed healthy before. A seizure, the inability of a heart to pump, the sudden deterioration of muscle tone in a small child—being unable to reverse such conditions or even to understand why they occur was unspeakably frustrating to healers. Even before there were names for such conditions, even before they were understood at all, each was a reminder of how complex the human body is, and how vulnerable.

While our grappling with understanding diseases has been frustrating at times, it has also provided some of humankind's most heroic accomplishments. Alexander Fleming's accidental discovery in 1928 of a mold that could be turned into penicillin has resulted in the saving of untold millions of lives. The isolation of the enzyme insulin has reversed what was once a death sentence for anyone with diabetes. There have been great strides in combating conditions for which there is not yet a cure, too. Medicines can help AIDS patients live longer, diagnostic tools such as mammography and ultrasound can help doctors find tumors while they are treatable, and laser surgery techniques have made the most intricate, minute operations routine.

This "toe-to-toe" competition with diseases and disorders is even more remarkable when seen in a historical continuum. An astonishing amount of progress has been made in a very short time. Just two hundred years ago, the existence of germs as a cause of some diseases was unknown. In fact, it was less than 150 years ago that a British surgeon named Joseph Lister had difficulty persuading his fellow doctors that washing their hands before delivering a baby might increase the chances of a healthy delivery (especially if they had just attended to a diseased patient)!

Each book in Lucent's *Diseases and Disorders* series explores a disease or disorder and the knowledge that has been accumulated (or discarded) by doctors through the years. Each book also examines the tools used for pinpointing a diagnosis, as well as the various means that are used to treat or cure a disease. Finally, new ideas are presented—techniques or medicines that may be on the horizon.

Frustration and disappointment are still part of medicine, for not every disease or condition can be cured or prevented. But the limitations of knowledge are being pushed outward constantly; the "most difficult puzzles ever devised" are finding challengers every day.

A Neurological Syndrome

JOSH WAS DIAGNOSED with attention deficit disorder (ADD) in second grade. In school he found himself daydreaming instead of listening attentively. No matter how hard he tried, he couldn't direct his attention back to the teacher or make himself focus on the task at hand. He was always restless. Sitting quietly and listening was almost impossible. Even though he knew he wasn't supposed to, he felt compelled to move around and talk. Little things made him angry, and he frequently got into fights with the other children. "I was totally out of control," he recalls. Josh's parent took him to his pediatrician, who, with the help of other experts, diagnosed Josh with ADD. "My doctor explained that I'd probably have ADD for the rest of my life. Chances are I'd never outgrow it, but with the right treatment I could live a normal life." That was ten years ago. Josh's doctor was right. Today Josh is a happy high school senior who dreams of winning a college scholarship and becoming a psychologist. "Now that I've got my ADD under control nothing can stop me,"[1] he says.

People with the disorder generally have greater-than-average problems focusing their attention, are extremely restless, and often are impulsive. ADD experts Dr. Edward M. Hallowell and Dr. John J. Ratey explain: "ADD is a neurological syndrome that is usually genetically transmitted. It is characterized by impulsiveness, distractibility, and restlessness. The symptoms are present from childhood with greater intensity than in the average person, so they interfere with daily functions."[2]

Most people exhibit restlessness, distraction, and impulsiveness at one time or another. For this reason, there is controversy

8

A young boy with attention deficit disorder works to solve a math problem. People with ADD have a difficult time focusing their attention and as a result often struggle in school.

over whether ADD is an actual disorder or whether it is just a symptom of the increasingly hectic pace of life in the twenty-first century. What distinguishes people with ADD for the rest of the population is that they exhibit these symptoms to a much greater degree than others do.

If there is controversy over whether ADD even exists, there is also disagreement over what causes the disorder. There has been a lot of research on the subject, with contradictory findings. Some researchers contend that chemical imbalances in the brain cause the symptoms collectively known as ADD. Others believe that the brains of those with ADD are actually structured differently.

What is not open to question is that ADD presents a problem for society. Although attention deficit disorder does not attract the media coverage that other illnesses and medical conditions get, it affects about 15 million people in the United States. Inattention and restlessness cause difficulty for students in school, and workers to suffer from loss of productivity on the job. Problems with impulsiveness can lead to a wide variety of socially disruptive and often dangerous behaviors, including criminal activity. In addition, personal relationships often suffer. Although people with ADD may know what they should do in social situations, they may find themselves unable to control the impulse to behave inappropriately.

Because of the serious implications of ADD both for its victims and for society in general, researchers are working hard to learn more about the disorder in hopes of finding exactly what causes ADD, how to treat it more effectively, and a way to cure it. To understand this disorder, however, it is necessary to look to the past.

Chapter 1

A Misunderstood Problem

THE TERM *ATTENTION deficit disorder* was first used in the 1970s but the disorder has existed much longer under different names, each of which represents a different view of the disorder. Terms such as *restlessness disorder, minimal brain dysfunction,* and *hyperkinetic impulse disorder* all referred to a set of symptoms variously thought to be caused by bad blood, demonic possession, nervousness, immorality, a disordered nervous system, bad parenting, vitamin deficiency, sugar consumption, or food additives.

Regardless of what ADD was called, doctors even in ancient times puzzled over the disorder. Around 400 B.C. the Greek physician Hippocrates hypothesized that the symptoms known today as ADD were caused by an imbalance in the four bodily humors that were thought to control human health and personality: phlegm, blood, yellow bile, and black bile. Hippocrates and his contemporaries were not, however, successful in treating the condition.

Since ancient times, doctors such as the Greek physician Hippocrates (pictured) have come up with a variety of theories to explain what causes the symptoms of ADD.

The more than two millennia that followed saw no progress in understanding ADD and its sufferers. During the Middle Ages, for example, it was commonly thought that people who acted differently, including those with disabilities involving learning, were possessed by the devil. Prayers were said for the afflicted, and they were given herbal preparations in an effort to purge the devil from their bodies. Those who failed to improve were often chained up and locked away for the rest of their lives. Surgery, which involved drilling a hole in the patient's skull in order to let the devil escape, was performed on others. In an age when nobody understood the need for sanitation of any kind, the results were usually a quick, unpleasant death for the patient. As a final solution, some sufferers were burned alive to kill the devil inside of them.

By the 1800s the belief that differences in behavior were caused by demonic possession had given way to a new belief that such behavior was inborn—the result of the immoral behavior of the patient's parents and grandparents. Behavior that did not fit the norm was believed to run in families and to be common among certain ethnic groups. Despite this belief in heredity, it was commonly accepted that children exhibiting ADD-like symptoms were acting willfully and could easily change if they wanted to. It was believed that severe punishment, which included frequent beatings, would lead the offender to become more attentive and change his or her behavior. Books on child rearing described various methods of beating children and implored parents to do so. Other treatments included herbs, hypnotism, and religious devotion.

The nineteenth century saw modest progress as some doctors began to focus on the central nervous system in their search for a cause of ADD. By the middle of the 1800s ADD-like symptoms were diagnosed as being caused by nervousness. Excessive nervousness, in turn, was believed to be a direct result of eating spicy food, overwork, immoral living, and/or overuse of the brain. Treatment included a bland diet, bed rest, and Bible study. People with extreme symptoms were committed to insane asylums, where, historians explain, "treatment consisted of labor, spiritual and cultural improvement, nutrition, education and exercise."[3] These treatments were believed to physically and spiritually cleanse the patient, thus eliminating problems with extreme nervousness.

The Disordered Nervous System

The idea that mental problems were the result of some sort of malfunction in the central nervous system finally took hold toward the end of the nineteenth century. William James, one of the earliest American psychologists, studied people with deficits in what he called "inhibitory volition, moral control, and sustained attention."[4] As James described them, these deficits bore a close resemblance to the currently accepted symptoms of ADD: impulsiveness, restlessness, and distractibility. These and other symptoms, such as insomnia, irritability, and tiredness, were lumped together under the general diagnosis of neurasthenia. James suggested that these deficits were caused by a neurological defect in the brain. Initial treatment included special diet, ex-

Nineteenth-century psychologist William James believed that the symptoms of ADD were the result of a neurological defect in the brain.

ercise, and bed rest. It was also thought that the nervous systems of people who suffered from neurasthenia were sluggish and needed stimulation. To rectify this problem, patients were treated with very low doses of electrical shock. Other treatments common at this time included enemas, thus ridding patients of whatever ailed them. Various types of water therapy, which involved immersing the patient in hot and cold baths, were also used. This therapy was believed to comfort and calm patients, especially those who were hyperactive.

Blame the Parents

While William James was looking at the brain itself for clues to behavior problems, others were looking at the thoughts produced by the brain. In the 1890s the Austrian physician Sigmund Freud theorized that all mental disorders, including ADD-like problems, were caused by repressed memories of emotional traumas. Freud believed that parents who were extremely nervous, overly protective, indulgent, or emotionally distant could cause their children to display symptoms such as distractibility, impulsiveness, and restlessness. By allowing a patient to talk freely in a process he called free association, Freud believed that memory of the trauma would surface and this recollection would lead to a cure. Freud's psychoanalysis treatment regimen remained a common treatment for symptoms of attention deficit disorder for many years.

Evidence that Freud and others were unfairly blaming parents for ADD-like symptoms soon surfaced, however. In 1902 George Frederick Still, a British pediatrician, studied a group of children who exhibited behaviors that caused Still to say they were "defiant, excessively emotional, passionate, lawless, spiteful, and had little inhibitory volition."[5] Still investigated these children's families—believing that he would find bad parenting as the cause of the children's problems—but was surprised to find that these children were raised by parents who followed commonly accepted rules for child rearing. As a

Sigmund Freud attributed all mental disorders, including ADD-like symptoms, to repressed memories of childhood emotional trauma.

result, Still theorized that these children's problems were biological in origin. Finding that some of the children's relatives suffered from a variety of mental disorders, Still postulated that the cause of the children's problems was as likely to be biological in nature as it was to be social.

Further evidence for a biological basis for attention deficit disorder's behavioral symptoms came a few years later during a major outbreak of encephalitis, an inflammation of the brain. After recovering from encephalitis, many patients exhibited such symptoms as being easily distracted, impulsive, and overactive. In 1934 psychologists Eugene Kahn and Louis Cohen named this disorder "organic driveness" and theorized that it was a result of brain damage caused by the infection.

Relief Is Provided by Stimulants

At the same time, Charles Bradley, an American physician, also theorized that ADD-like symptoms were caused by a problem in the brain. Bradley studied and worked with children who exhibited the same symptoms as the subjects of Kahn and Cohen's study. These children experienced difficulty concentrating, behavioral problems, and difficulty sitting still. As a group, these youngsters were doing quite poorly in school. In addition, a number of these children suffered from severe headaches that did not respond to medication. Bradley tried treating their headaches with the stimulant Benzedrine, hoping it would provide relief. Although the Benzedrine was not an effective painkiller, it had the surprising effect of relieving his patients' ADD-like symptoms.

Bradley could not explain why a stimulant would help these children. Logically, it would seem that it would only worsen their problems with restlessness, for example. According to Bradley, the medication worked "in a spectacular fashion."[6] He hypothesized that in some way the medication stimulated the part of the brain that inhibited activity.

By the 1940s physicians, psychologists, and psychiatrists realized that different people exhibited different levels of intensity of what was then called restlessness syndrome or organic driveness. Based on Still's theories that these ailments were biologically caused, doctors believed that severe levels of the illness were caused by brain damage. However, these researchers continued to blame poor parenting for milder cases of the ailment.

By the 1950s the disorder, now known to experts as *minimal brain dysfunction* and later as *minimal brain disorder,* was believed to be caused by a defect in the nervous system. Still, symptoms were commonly treated with psychoanalysis, partly because of the strong faith therapists placed in Freud's theories and partly because Bradley's successful work with stimulants was not widely known.

Drugs Provide Some Relief

By the 1960s parents, educators, and researchers had focused their attention on one aspect of ADD: the inability of some children to sit still. Thanks to this widely shared trait, minimal brain disorder became widely known as *hyperactive child syndrome, hyperkinetic reaction,* or *hyperkinetic impulse disorder.*

A six-year-old with ADD expends some of his energy on the playground. Children with ADD are often hyperactive and have difficulty sitting still.

At the same time, Bradley's work with stimulants proved the basis for the first medication aimed at controlling hyperactive behavior. Known by its brand name, Ritalin, this drug provided some relief to those with ADD. Still, other symptoms, such as difficulty concentrating, are even more common than hyperactivity.

An Ongoing Search

Despite the absence of conclusive evidence pointing to a single cause, by the 1980s ADD was firmly established as a recognized disorder. Aware of the need to help physicians diagnose the disorder, the American Psychiatric Association for the first time published official guidelines in its standard reference, the *Diagnostic and Statistical Manual of Mental Disorders*. Although the term *attention deficit disorder* had been used previously to describe the disorder, it was in this publication that the term was first officially used. These guidelines remain the most commonly used tool for diagnosing attention deficit disorder.

Meanwhile, researchers have continued working to understand the nature of ADD in hopes of developing better treatments. In 1975, for example, allergy expert Dr. Benjamin Feingold theorized that artificial flavorings and preservatives in food marketed to children were causing them to be hyperactive. Feingold speculated that hyperactivity and attention deficit symptoms were allergic reactions to these chemicals. Feingold developed a strict diet that he believed would cure children of ADD. Although the diet was prescribed for many patients with the disorder and a few seemed to improve, the majority did not. In fact, no proof was ever found that diet or allergies of any kind cause ADD.

Efforts to link diet to attention deficit disorder continued, however. Dr. Ronald Prinz hypothesized that poor attention, hyperactivity, and aggressive behavior in children were caused by too much sugar in their diet. Prinz conducted a study that showed that, in some cases, these symptoms did improve when sugar was removed from the subjects' diets. Although the results were not conclusive, many people continue to believe that sugar negatively affects behavior, and many parents try to limit the sugar consumption of their children with attention deficit disorder.

ADD expert Thom Hartmann points to the difficulty of pin-pointing a single culprit for the disorder: "ADD children and adults often report an inordinate craving for sugar. They may also be sensitive to the highs and crashes that come from sugar, alcohol, caffeine, and illicit drug consumption (and may benefit from avoiding these substances). But these sensitivities may have little or nothing to do with symptoms of a disease."[7]

Out of the Darkness

Growing awareness of attention deficit disorder and its impact on society has led to more extensive funding for research into the workings of the brain with regard to people with the disorder. The development of scanning and imaging devices such as magnetic resonance imaging (MRI) made it possible to examine the brains of people with ADD to search for biological causes of the disorder.

Some doctors believe that a high-sugar diet contributes to aggressive behavior, poor attention, and hyperactivity, all of which are common symptoms of ADD.

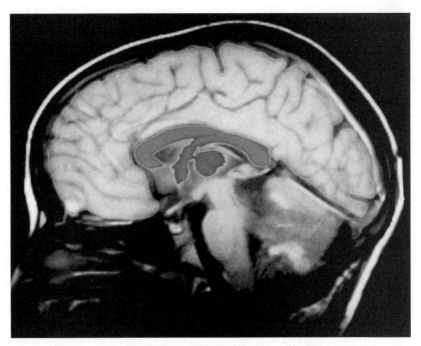

The search for a biological cause of ADD has been aided by magnetic resonance imaging (MRI), which makes it possible to examine the brains of living people who have the disorder.

A complete understanding of the causes of ADD continues to elude researchers, and since ADD is not a condition that someone outgrows, those with the condition must hope that a cure is someday found. Nonetheless, understanding and acceptance is helping those with attention deficit disorder cope with its effects. Ongoing research into the human brain should yield greater understanding and possibly a cure.

Chapter 2

Causes and Diagnosis

D ESPITE EXTENSIVE RESEARCH, nobody knows exactly what causes ADD. Although none are conclusive, the most commonly accepted theories are that attention deficit disorder is caused by imbalances in the chemicals that control brain activities and/or a structural difference in the brains of those suffering from ADD. Most researchers believe, furthermore, that these abnormalities are the result of genetic flaws rather than some kind of brain injury.

The brain is the focus of a great deal of the research being done today on ADD, as many experts believe the disorder is caused by abnormalities or chemical imbalances in this vital organ.

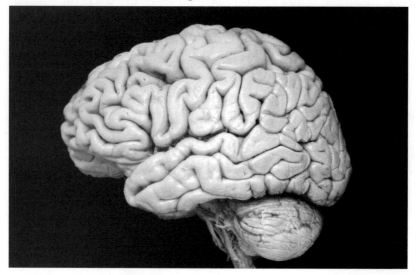

20

Chemical Imbalance of Neurotransmitters

Research has shown that the cells of the human brain rely on chemicals known as neurotransmitters to form thoughts, store and retrieve information, and translate thoughts and memories into physical actions. Research has shown that in the brains of at least some people with ADD, one of these neurotransmitters, dopamine, is found in abnormally low amounts. Animal research appears to confirm the connection between dopamine and ADD. Research conducted on monkeys demonstrated that when dopamine levels were decreased, both memory and attentiveness were diminished. Since problems with memory and attention are experienced by people with ADD, many researchers believe that decreased levels of dopamine may be responsible. Moreover, research has indicated that in 60 percent of ADD sufferers, the genes controlling dopamine production are in some way abnormal.

Structural Differences

Not everyone with attention deficit disorder suffers from low dopamine levels, however, and other research has shown that there appear to be structural differences in the forebrain of some people with the disorder. The forebrain is the part of the brain that controls thoughts, behavior, and emotions. It controls the ability to reason, solve problems, and make decisions. One part of the forebrain, the frontal lobe, is most involved with memory, thought, motivation, judgment, perseverance, and behavior. Research has shown that some children with ADD have forebrains about 10 percent smaller than children who do not suffer from ADD. In addition, blood flow to the frontal lobe is diminished in these children, which some experts believe means that the activity level is reduced in just that part of the brain responsible for focusing and maintaining attention, controlling emotions, and persevering at difficult tasks.

Another structural difference found in the forebrains of some people with ADD involves the corpus callosum. The corpus callosum has been shown to be responsible for allowing the left and right hemispheres of the brain to communicate with each other. When this communication is impeded, the result is inattentiveness.

Children with ADD appear to have smaller-than-average corpus callosam, so researchers speculate that the inattention they display may be the result of this smaller structure.

A third structural difference has been observed in the basal ganglia, which is also located in the forebrain. Among its various functions, the basal ganglia is responsible for controlling a person's sense of time. Studies have found that the basal ganglia in some people with ADD is smaller than normal and less active. Researchers believe this could cause the problems these people experience in dealing with time management. Moreover, the fact that the basal ganglia controls sleep patterns, coupled with the fact that those with ADD commonly suffer from sleep disturbances, suggests a connection.

Because various studies have established a number of possible culprits, research into the cause of attention deficit disorder continues. Meanwhile, other researchers are concentrating on improving the tools needed to identify people with ADD.

Diagnosis: An Inexact Science

Because no one physical cause of ADD has been identified, there is no medical test to aid in identifying those with attention deficit disorder. In the absence of a diagnostic test, an accurate diagnosis relies on a person's clinical history. Adding to the diagnostic problems, almost everyone experiences ADD-like symptoms at some time, resulting in ongoing problems with misdiagnosis. According to Dr. Edward M. Hallowell and Dr. John Ratey, "There is no clear line of demarcation between ADD and normal behavior. Rather, one must make a judgement based on a comparison of an individual to his or her peer group."[8] In order to be considered truly suffering from ADD, one must experience ADD-like symptoms with more intensity and for a longer duration than the average person. But ADD symptoms range from mild to extreme, making objective assessment difficult.

"A Very Thin Line"

Complicating the diagnostic picture is the problem of differentiating normal behavior from ADD behavior, particularly in very

Diagnosis of ADD is especially difficult because people suffering from other psychiatric disorders, such as depression, experience some ADD-like symptoms.

young children. "Lucas has always been a firecracker," one parent explains.

> When he started nursery school, his teacher suggested we have him tested for ADD because he just couldn't sit still in the reading circle and was always bothering the other children. Our pediatrician warned us that there's a very thin line between normal behavior and ADD behavior in a three-year-old. He thought that Lucas's problem was probably immaturity and told us to wait until Lucas was at least six to have him tested, which we never had to do. Lucas just seemed to outgrow the whole thing.[9]

Further problems with misdiagnosis occur when the symptoms of other disorders are mistaken for ADD and vice versa. Attention deficit disorder expert Dr. Lawrence H. Diller explains: "ADD, as officially described, can look a lot like certain other childhood psychiatric disorders. And many children meet criteria for some, but not all, of the symptoms for several different conditions."[10] This is also the case for adults. Problems such as depression, seasonal mood disorder, anxiety disorder, schizophrenia, Tourette's syndrome, obsessive-compulsive disorder, oppositional defiant disorder, conduct disorder, and bipolar disorder all exhibit ADD-like symptoms.

In fact, distractibility, restlessness, and impulsivity are so common in anxiety disorders and depression that, according to mental health expert Dr. Larry B. Silver, "ADHD [as ADD is sometimes called] is the least likely cause." However, "many diagnosticians do not consider these possibilities when confronted with a patient with distractibility, impulsiveness and restlessness, automatically diagnosing the problem as ADHD."[11] Furthermore, problems with hearing and sight, which could be the cause of inattentiveness, as well as other medical conditions such as thyroid problems or lead poisoning, also often mimic ADD symptoms.

Children with various psychological problems exhibit many of the symptoms of ADD, and are often misdiagnosed as a result.

In addition to mental illnesses, certain traits displayed by gifted people also can be mistaken for attention deficit disorder. Like ADD sufferers, gifted people often seem inattentive, but their inattentiveness is due to boredom. Gifted children may also appear restless due to their high energy levels. In fact, one gifted child, who graduated from college at age ten, was initially diagnosed with ADD when he was a toddler and treatment with Ritalin was prescribed. As it happened, his parents did not believe their son's inattention was caused by ADD and refused treatment. The youngster's father notes, "Children like Michael have an attention surplus. He's so much faster than we are. In two seconds he's figured out what you are going to say. He's toyed with a few answers and now he's looking around waiting for you to finish. It looks like he's not paying attention and it drives teachers crazy."[12]

Some experts are concerned that since the ADD diagnosis focuses almost entirely on the individual, family problems are often overlooked. This is particularly true among children and teenagers, who may be dealing with serious problems at home such as a sick or abusive parent. One ADD specialist explains that a child with family problems "daydreams, cannot focus, and worries a lot about the future. In the classroom, this child can look like he has ADHD."[13]

Because ADD is so often mistaken for other conditions, many people move through life without their disorder ever being correctly diagnosed. According to Hallowell and Ratey, "Many adults who have ADD do not suspect they have it. They just feel that something is amiss in some unnameable way. Many are being treated for some condition other than ADD, the ADD lying masked and undetected."[14] In fact, studies have shown that two out of three people with ADD will never be diagnosed. And the opposite problem also occurs: People who suffer from other physical and mental disorders are sometimes falsely diagnosed with ADD.

Yet another source of misdiagnosis is simple lack of expertise among health care providers. The guidelines set by the American Psychiatric Association's *Diagnostic and Statistical Manual of Mental Disorders (DSM IV)* may be a physician's only diagnostic tool. *DSM IV*'s checklist of symptomatic behaviors, their intensity, and their frequency, without further details or investigation, is often in-adequate for accurate diagnosis. According to one ADD expert, "Of-ficial guidelines for evaluating ADD symptoms are vague and open to interpretation—yet they lead to an all-or-nothing diagnosis."[15]

Because of the problems with diagnosing ADD, evaluation by a psychologist, psychiatrist, or other physician remains the vital first step in dealing with ADD, or attention deficit hyperactivity disorder (ADHD), as it is technically called. An interview with the patient and with family members and/or teachers begins the evaluation process. IQ and other tests are given to rule out other learning disabilities and mental disorders, and medical tests are used to determine that the patient's symptoms are not being caused by a physical problem. After other possible causes of the symptoms have been ruled out, the patient's symptoms are eval-uated according to guidelines published in *DSM IV.*

Although many people speak of ADD or ADHD as though it is a single disorder, these terms actually refer to a group of three related conditions, and the professional evaluating the patient must narrow the diagnosis accordingly. Ironically, despite its

An accurate diagnosis of ADD must include a thorough evaluation by a doctor and a detailed interview with the patient, family members, and often teachers.

One type of ADD is characterized by inattention without symptoms of hyperactivity. People with this type of ADD are easily distracted and are often dismissed as being daydreamers.

technical medical name, one major type of ADD (or ADHD) does not include symptoms of hyperactivity. Instead, the dominant symptom is inattention. People with this type of ADD are usually easily distracted. As a result, they are usually poor listeners. They are often disorganized and lose things easily, tend to be forgetful, and often have trouble finishing tasks. To a casual observer, these people appear to be daydreamers. For reasons that are unclear, more females than males suffer from this type of ADD. These people are usually quiet and mild mannered, and since they rarely cause any trouble, they often remain undiagnosed for most of their lives.

The second subtype, ADHD without inattention, is the least common type of the disorder. The dominant symptom is hyperactivity and impulsiveness. This form is more common among males than females, again for unknown reasons. Sufferers tend to be extremely restless and seem unable to sit still. They tend to talk excessively and may have frequent outbursts. They are impatient, experience frequent mood swings, and often exhibit aggressive behavior. These sufferers also frequently have problems controlling their temper. Because of their highly visible symptoms, people with this form of ADD are usually referred to doctors at a young age.

The third subtype, ADHD with inattention, hyperactivity, and impulsiveness, is the most common type of the disorder. This form combines the symptoms of the other two subtypes; again for unknown reasons, it more frequently afflicts males than females.

Making the correct diagnosis is often challenging, but once that happens, the results can be liberating. According to Hallowell and Ratey, "More than most other disorders, often just making a diagnosis of ADD exerts a powerful therapeutic effect. The walls of years of misunderstanding come crashing down."[16]

Chapter 3

Treatment

A S IS TRUE of diagnosis, treatment of attention deficit disorder is complex and inexact. In the absence of firm evidence of what causes ADD, treatment is difficult to prescribe. Moreover, no single treatment is effective for every patient, and doctors are unable to predict what treatment will be the best for a patient. Some treatments, such as the use of stimulants like Ritalin, have been proven effective in research studies, and they have been used to treat the symptoms of ADD for almost fifty years. Exactly how these medications work on the patient's body is still not completely understood. This has led to controversy about their safety for long-term use. There is also concern about possible side effects.

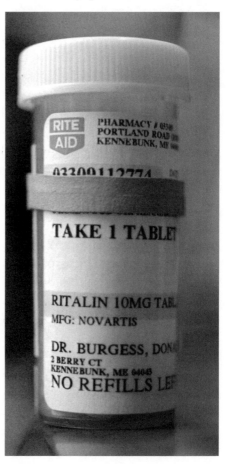

Although drugs such as Ritalin have been proven effective for many ADD sufferers, they do not work for everyone and there is concern about their long-term safety and side effects.

29

A Matter of Trial and Error

As is true of other therapies, no single medication is effective on everyone. In some cases, stimulants have no effect on symptoms and a physician will prescribe antidepressant medications instead. Whatever medication proves effective, finding the proper dosage may take weeks or even months of trial and error.

Because no single therapy works for everyone with ADD, some experts believe that combining a variety of treatments is often most effective. Such combined treatments require a cooperative effort between the patient, the patient's family, and the health care professional. When successful, these combined treatments will relieve many of the symptoms of ADD.

Multimodal Treatment

Combining a variety of treatments to treat ADD is known as a multimodal approach. Although the number of people involved, along with the time and expense, make this approach impractical for some patients, studies have shown it to be effective. A multimodal approach generally involves behavioral therapy, psychotherapy or counseling, ADD coaching, and medication. Because so many different areas of expertise are involved, a multimodal treatment requires a team of professionals working with the patient. However, the first and most important person on the treatment team is the patient. It is important that adult and adolescent patients educate themselves about their condition and that children are told truthfully as much about the disorder as they can understand. Understanding their own situation helps patients to overcome negative self-perceptions, gain self-confidence, and develop coping skills that will help them live with the disorder. According to ADD experts Edward M. Hallowell and John J. Ratey, "Effective treatment often requires a radical rethinking of your view of yourself."[17]

Patients also find that it is important to educate those close to them because of the impact the disorder has on their personal, academic, and vocational life. Hallowell and Ratey advise ADD sufferers, "Educate and involve others. Just as it is key for you to understand ADD, it is equally if not more important for those

A kindergarten student with ADD gets encouragement from his teacher. In order for students with ADD to receive the special assistance they need, it is important for their teachers to be informed of the diagnosis.

around you to understand it—family, job, school, friends. Once they get the concept, they will be able to understand you much better and to help you reach your goals."[18] Helping these pivotal people in the patient's life to learn about ADD can prevent or rectify a number of misunderstandings. It can help a spouse or friend realize that their loved one is not ignoring them when he or she is inattentive. It can assist teachers to understand that a hyperactive child is not being purposefully rude or defiant when he or she refuses to stay quietly seated. Of course, once they are aware of a student's condition, teachers can develop an individual educational plan to meet his or her needs. Most importantly, learning about ADD will help make these people part of the multimodal treatment team.

The Multimodal Team

The members of the multimodal team are vital to the success of the patient's treatment. For children and adolescents with ADD, teachers, school counselors, psychologists, and parents work

A nine-year-old with ADD practices the keyboard while his parents watch. Parental involvement is considered the most crucial aspect of the multimodal team approach to treating ADD.

together to help them develop the necessary skills for coping with academic work, interpersonal relations, and day-to-day life. The importance of parental involvement in the multimodal team cannot be overemphasized. As one parent explains, "We took our son for psychological consultations, and we went for parental counseling. It's really helped us to know how to react to his overreactions."[19]

Structuring

The actual therapies employed by the team members are as varied as the ADD patients, but one of the most important techniques in the multimodal approach is the use of structuring. Structuring involves teaching someone with ADD to keep lists, carry notepads, write themselves reminders, keep appointment books and calendars, make schedules, save receipts, keep a bulletin board, and use computer systems, answering machines, or card files. This is done to help the ADD patient become organized, which is often extremely difficult. Although structuring uses common organization tools, many people with ADD have difficulty using them and must be assisted in their use at the beginning. According to Hallowell and Ratey, "People with ADD can spend a lifetime dodging the necessity of organizing themselves. They avoid getting organized the way some people avoid going to the dentist: repeatedly postponing it as the problem gets worse and worse. The task of getting organized, one that bedevils us all, particularly vexes the ADD mind."[20] Experts believe that when structuring is effective, it boosts the patient's self-esteem and self-confidence.

Coaching

Another part of multimodal treatment is coaching. The ADD coach is usually a counselor, psychologist, or therapist. However, the coach can also be a spouse, friend, or family member committed to encouraging and helping the ADD patient. The job of the coach is to help the person with ADD better cope with the disorder. ADD coach David Brown explains: "Coaches help their clients create an individualized structure and a best-fit environment that compensates externally for what is weak internally. As a coach my job is to facilitate goals and serve as a catalyst for achieving these goals."[21] Coaches do this by assisting with structuring and helping clients to maintain focus. They act as partners, encouraging those with ADD to do their best.

Other Behavioral Therapies

In addition to structuring, a number of other behavioral therapies are also used by psychologists and counselors. One such therapy is social-skills training. Social-skills training helps people with attention deficit disorder to become more socially adept. Often persons with ADD have trouble holding conversations because of their problem with inattention, so one skill that is developed is the ability to start and carry on a conversation. Another skill ADD patients learn is how to make and maintain eye contact, which helps to better focus their attention. Also, ADD patients are trained to wait their turn in a conversation rather than interrupting repeatedly or blurting out irrelevant comments.

Another approach that is often used with children is known as *cognitive behavioral therapy*. In this therapy, children with ADD learn a set of rules about their behavior and actions. They are taught through role-playing, workbooks, and talks with a counselor or therapist. The child's behavior and actions are recorded on a large chart which is posted in the home, and rewards are given for appropriate behavior and actions. The goal of this therapy is to help children with ADD become aware of what behavior is socially acceptable and what is not, and to eventually develop enough awareness to monitor their own behavior.

Sometimes, a psychotherapist is part of the multimodal team. Many people with ADD live with constant frustration, anxiety, and feelings of failure. Because of this, they develop a variety of emotional and psychological problems. These problems are usually best dealt with by individual psychotherapy sessions. Although not all ADD sufferers need psychotherapy, it has been shown to be an effective part of multimodal treatment, especially with adults and older adolescents.

Psychotherapy is often helpful in relieving symptoms of anxiety, frustration, and feelings of failure that people with ADD often experience.

To Medicate or Not to Medicate

A full multimodal approach to treating ADD includes medication in addition to structuring, coaching, behavioral therapy, and/or psychotherapy. However, out of concern about side effects or long-term consequences of using medications, some patients opt to try multimodal treatment without medication first. As one father explains, "When our doctor wanted to prescribe Ritalin, our answer was absolutely not. There aren't enough studies to know what it could do to you in later years, and there are other alternatives. We figured we'd try them all until we found something that worked."[22]

Some patients view medication as a crutch and prefer to try to control their symptoms without what they consider artificial assistance. According to Hallowell and Ratey,

> Very often at the initial stage of treatment there is a great reluctance to try medication. Parents do not want to "drug" their child, or the adult with ADD wants to make it on his own, without the aid of some unknown medication. Children, particularly boys, often feel that taking medicine is like admitting something scary is wrong with them. It may take months, even years before a child—or an adult—is ready to give medication a try.[23]

Oddly, although researchers know that medications like Ritalin (known generically as methylphenidate) work, they do not know exactly how they work. Most believe that the drug stimulates the production of neurotransmitters in the brain. Psychostimulants like Ritalin help about 80 percent of the patients who try it, but they do not work on everyone. Likewise, there is no way to predict who will be helped by the medication. For those people it helps, it is effective in the short term in sharpening their focus and decreasing impulsiveness, which improves their ability to concentrate. Researchers acknowledge there is no evidence that taking Ritalin will lead to any permanent improvement in the patient's symptoms. Once a patient stops taking Ritalin, any positive effects it had disappears.

Even for people who find relief with medication, there is a catch: Using a drug like Ritalin requires careful attention, which is exactly what someone with attention deficit disorder lacks. One common problem, then, is that patients forget to take their medication. Many people with ADD depend on friends and family members to remind them to take their medication. As one ADD sufferer explains, "When I was younger my mom handed me my medicine every morning. The nurse sent for me at school, and then my mom made sure I took it again at night. Now that I don't live with my mom any more, I only take my medicine once a day. But she calls me every morning to make sure I remember to take it."[24]

"When I Take It, I'm Calmer"

When treatment with Ritalin or other psychostimulants is effective, patients are able to focus and maintain their attention better for longer periods. They also have more control over their impulsiveness and restlessness. According to one person with ADD, "When I don't take my medicine, I get hyper. Without it, it's like I have millions of ideas going through my head, so I start talking really fast. I get distracted. I start doing one thing, and wind up going off and doing something else. When I take it, I'm calmer. I'm able to think better."[25] When it is beneficial, medication increases the user's sense of well-being. This helps boost the patient's self-confidence and self-esteem.

As with many medications, those meant to treat ADD have side effects. Among the most common of these are insomnia and loss of appetite. Insomnia is a common problem because the medication is a stimulant, and even though an ADD patient experiences some relief from restlessness, some disturbance of sleep patterns is possible. This problem can often be solved if the patient takes the last dose of medication in the late afternoon. This allows all traces of the medication to be out of the patient's body before bedtime.

Similarly, the other common side effect of stimulants is the loss of appetite. People taking Ritalin and other psychostimulants frequently suffer from lack of appetite, which often leads to weight

A six-year-old with ADD reads a book. Ritalin and other drugs help many ADD sufferers to focus and maintain their attention better.

loss and sometimes to the development of eating disorders. One ADD sufferer describes her brother, who has the disorder, in this way: "My brother is really thin. He takes his medicine before he eats, so he barely ever eats anything."[26] The problem of poor appetite may also cause young patients who take stimulants to experience slow growth patterns. Although experts do not believe this slowing is permanent, the use of these medications by younger children is controversial.

Ironically, another fairly common side effect of using medication is what occurs if the patient stops taking the drugs. When the medication wears off, even more severe symptoms of ADD often appear in some patients. These patients talk constantly and become very excitable, extremely hyperactive, and irritable. In addition, they often suffer from headaches and stomachaches. Changing the patient's medication schedule or dosage can sometimes rectify this problem. Taking a slow-release form of Ritalin also can be helpful in counteracting the rebound effect.

Some people with ADD complain that even though medication calms them and helps them to focus, it changes their personalities and inhibits their creativity. ADD expert Thom Hartmann explains how this affected one ADD sufferer: "He found that Ritalin, while smoothing out his emotional swings, stabilizing his time-sense, and giving him the ability to concentrate on his work, also took away a bit of his spontaneity, humor, and sense of the absurd, which he enjoyed."[27]

A more troubling side effect of Ritalin is the possible development of facial tics and other symptoms of Tourette's syndrome, a neurological disorder. People who exhibit this problem must discontinue treatment with Ritalin, although the tics may persist for several months before disappearing.

For adults, there is yet another serious side effect: high blood pressure. Since high blood pressure can lead to heart attacks and strokes, patients who experience this side effect must be closely monitored if they choose to continue the medication.

Controversial Long-Term Effects

Although Ritalin and other psychostimulants have been in use for decades, few long-term studies have been done on the continual use of these medications. With this in mind, many people with ADD refuse treatment with medication out of concern about possible long-term side effects. Among the most disturbing and most controversial of these is the possibility that treatment with psychostimulants will eventually lead to drug abuse in some patients. Research has shown that some people who have been treated with Ritalin and other psychostimulants for ADD are at

Some studies have shown that children with ADD who are treated with Ritalin and other stimulants are at greater risk of abusing drugs later in life.

risk of abusing drugs later in life. However, it is hard for researchers to determine whether early use of Ritalin is the cause of later drug abuse or if problems with drug abuse are simply caused by the risk-taking and impulsive behaviors that are symptomatic of ADD.

Some researchers worry that since Ritalin and other psychostimulants affect the levels of neurotransmitters in the brain, it is possible that, with long-term use, the brain may adjust its natural production of neurotransmitters downward to compensate. This could make long-term Ritalin users more prone to developing diseases that are caused by low neurotransmitter levels, such as Parkinson's and Alzheimer's, as they age.

Still another major concern is that high doses of Ritalin or the psychostimulant Dexedrine can produce a euphoric effect, causing these medications to be used as recreational drugs. According to ADD expert Dr. Lawrence H. Diller, "A recent report noted that an eleven-year-old boy was stealing his own medicine from his grandmother because the tablets made him feel 'nice,' and 'very happy.' Another patient was caught by his father taking an extra tablet of Ritalin before playing football. He said it made him feel 'sharper.'"[28] Due to their euphoric effect, Ritalin and Dexedrine have been sold illegally in schools, clubs, and on the street, and the federal government's Drug Enforcement Administration (DEA) has identified a growing trend among school-age youngsters in Ritalin abuse.

Studies tend to confirm the DEA's concern. One reporter notes, "One national school survey conducted by the Institute of Social Research at the University of Michigan shows that in 1997, almost 3% of high school seniors were using Ritalin without a doctor's order. Another survey shows 7% of all Indiana high school students used Ritalin for non-medical reasons."[29]

Ritalin, Dexedrine, and Adderall are all psychostimulants, and when abused, they can have the same effect on the body. Overdoses of psychostimulants can cause hallucinations, seizures, stroke, high blood pressure, and blood clots in the heart and lungs, resulting in death. These potentially serious side effects associated with the use of these drugs have sparked controversy and doubt over the effectiveness and safety of their use as a treatment for ADD. Adding urgency to the debate is the fact that the federal Department of Health and Human Services reports a six-fold increase in emergency room visits due to Ritalin abuse between 1990 and 2000.

Alternative Treatments

The possible side effects of Ritalin and other psychostimulants have motivated many people with ADD and their families to search for alternatives. Among these are special diets designed to avoid foods and food additives such as dyes and preservatives, which some researchers claim cause the symptoms of ADD. These

First Lady Hillary Rodham Clinton and Surgeon General David Satcher announce the launch of a White House–sponsored effort to caution parents about giving their children Ritalin and other psychostimulants to treat ADD.

diets have not been proven to have any significant effect on relieving the symptoms of attention deficit disorder. Although a number of people believe avoiding certain foods has been effective in treating their ADD, some researchers attribute this effectiveness to a placebo effect in which the patient's belief in the diet actually contributes to its effectiveness. Other researchers point out that many people who suffer from food allergies exhibit ADD-like symptoms as a reaction to eating certain foods. For these people, these dietary changes might give positive results, but whether these people actually suffer from ADD is questionable. As Dr. Larry B. Silver explains, "There is a relationship between brain function and nutrition as well as between brain function and allergic reactions. There are no known treatments [for ADD] based on these relationships that are clinically successful."[30]

Others dealing with ADD look to herbal treatments as an alternative to medication. Herbs such as valerian, skullcap, and hops, which act as sedatives, have been used by ADD patients, as have stimulant herbs such as gingerroot and licorice. However, like other types of medication, some herbs can have serious side effects, and there have been few studies aimed at confirming their effectiveness. Use of the dietary supplement L-tyrosine, an amino acid that the body uses to synthesize dopamine, is also becoming increasingly popular, although little research has been done on this treatment.

Treatment of the physical, emotional, and mental symptoms of ADD with homeopathic remedies—microdoses of individually prescribed natural substances that are believed to cause the symptoms of the disorder being treated—has also gained popularity. Although some patients find relief with homeopathic treatment, there is no current evidence that this is anything more than the placebo effect at work.

Other treatments for ADD are even more questionable. Chiropractors, claiming that the spine of an ADD patient is not aligned correctly, offer spinal adjustments. Other practitioners, claiming that ADD sufferers have two misarranged bones in their skulls causing pressure on their brains, offer a treatment that involves

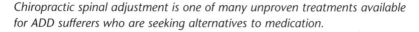

Chiropractic spinal adjustment is one of many unproven treatments available for ADD sufferers who are seeking alternatives to medication.

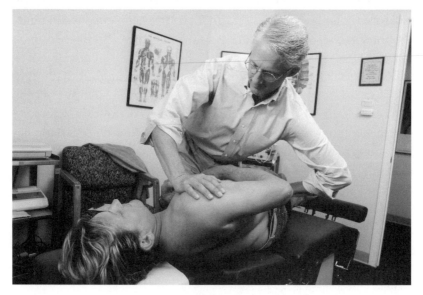

manipulating the bones of the skull and the area around the eyes. As with dietary treatments, there is no scientific evidence that these treatments are effective. Some people with ADD claim to have gotten relief from chiropractic treatment. Some researchers attribute this relief to the possibility that when the spine is correctly aligned, it enables the rest of the body to function more efficiently, thereby assisting in a more balanced production of chemicals in the brain.

One of the newest alternative treatments for ADD is the use of biofeedback. This treatment is based on the theory that people with attention deficit disorder have slow brain-wave patterns, causing inattention. Through biofeedback therapy, patients with ADD are trained to consciously increase the speed of their brain waves. Limited research has shown that treatment with biofeedback has a significant effect on improving the patient's problem with distractibility. However, there is not yet enough research data for definite proof that biofeedback is effective.

Because of a lack of knowledge about what causes ADD and how to definitively diagnose the disorder, it is difficult to determine what constitutes an appropriate and effective treatment. However, through trial and error, health professionals can help patients with attention deficit disorder to find treatments that will help them to live happier, more successful lives. Meanwhile, people with ADD—and those around them—make the best of a difficult situation.

Chapter 4

Problems with Few Solutions

THE FRUSTRATION OF coping with the symptoms of attention deficit disorder means that many ADD sufferers are at risk of developing a variety of short- and long-term psychological, emotional, and social problems. According to ADD experts Edward M. Hallowell and John J. Ratey, "These problems are the direct and unhappy result of years of frustration, failure or of just not getting it right. Even the person with ADD who has achieved a great deal usually feels in some way defective."[31]

People with ADD often develop secondary symptoms such as depression and low self-esteem, along with the accompanying

Years of coping with the frustrating symptoms of ADD causes many sufferers to develop poor self-esteem and a variety of psychological and social problems.

poor peer relationships. Undesirable behaviors, such as aggression, drug and alcohol abuse, and criminal activity, are also a frequent outgrowth of ADD's primary symptoms. For some whose symptoms go undiagnosed, the knowledge that they might have found help earlier only adds to their frustration. One ADD sufferer explains:

> I'm forty years old and I have wasted my life. If I'd known about ADD when I was in high school, and had had Ritalin then, I may have made it through. I might have graduated from college an honors student. I might be a successful professional now, instead of somebody who's had ten jobs in twenty years. I feel like my life has been totally wasted, and there's no way I can go back and recover those lost years.[32]

Social Problems

People with attention deficit disorder face a number of social problems. Many who have ADD spend much of their lives feeling different from everyone else and trying to hide their perceived differences. They frequently have problems making friends and developing and maintaining close relationships, resulting in feeling alienated and lonely. The ADD sufferer's tendency to fail to make eye contact, listen, or notice important social cues causes others to feel as if they are being snubbed or ignored. Of course, these are some of the classic symptoms of the disorder, and people with ADD have little control over them. As one ADD sufferer explains, "My mind is always wandering. I can't stay focused on one thing long. People think I'm not paying attention. They get all upset. They say, 'What's the matter with you? Don't you find me interesting?' instead of realizing it's not them or me, it's my ADD."[33]

Because those with ADD have problems noticing or understanding social cues such as body language, being part of a group is often difficult. According to ADD specialist Dr. Lawrence H. Diller, "They lack awareness of what is going on in a group and the effect of their behavior on the group. ADHD individuals don't read facial cues or body language and miss other social cues."[34]

This inability to function successfully as part of a group further isolates ADD sufferers. As one explains, "I'm terrified to go to a party. All the conversations going on around me, the constantly changing topics, the different personalities and styles . . . I simply get overwhelmed."[35]

Problems with restlessness also inhibit people with ADD from developing the social network most have access to. Their restlessness interferes with most normal social activities. According to one ADD sufferer, "I can't take a date to the movies or out to dinner. I'll tell her I have to go to the bathroom at least a half dozen times, when I really just have to go for a walk. I can't help it. I just have to go, go, go. Lots of women don't understand."[36]

The social problems that people with ADD face can be especially difficult for children, since they often do not understand why they are being rejected by their peers. The effect of this problem can be long-term and devastating. Psychologists Stephen W. Garber, Marianne Daniels Garber, and Robyn Freedman Spizman note, "Learning to live, work and play with others is crucial to a

Peer rejection and the resulting feelings of isolation can be especially painful for children with ADD.

happy life. Research indicates that children without friends, who are isolated from their peers, are at risk of continuing problems with their peers, poor academic achievement, and poor adjustment to school."[37]

Problems at School and at Work

For school-age children, the school environment can exacerbate the effects of ADD. As one individual with ADD recalls,

> I was tortured in school. A kid with ADD, the teacher would tell me to sit down, pay attention—it was torture. I'd hear the lights buzzing, the cars passing in the street, the teacher tapping her pencil. I was boiling and burning. I was always in trouble, always behind. I didn't intentionally drift off. I couldn't help myself. I spent all the time playing catch up.[38]

Unfortunately for the student with ADD, the qualities most necessary for successful performance in most schools—the ability to focus one's mind and to control one's own behavior—are the very qualities they often lack. In fact, studies have shown that students with the disorder are two to three times more likely to fail in school than other students. They tend to receive lower grades in their classes, score lower on achievement tests, and they may be one to two years behind in language arts and/or math. They are also more likely to drop out of high school than their peers are.

At Greater Risk of Learning Disabilities

In addition to the problems these students experience due to their ADD symptoms, approximately one-third of them also have learning disabilities. According to Garber, Garber, and Spizman, "A learning disability is defined as a problem in learning that is not a result of poor intelligence or poor teaching. The individual has average or above-average intelligence but fails to learn despite good instruction. A learning disability can severely block learning."[39] Learning disabilities diminish skills in specific subject areas such as math, spelling, or reading. They also intrude on a person's ability to learn, making him or her too preoccupied

A young boy with ADD in addition to a learning disability practices writing numbers with his special education teacher. The problems students with ADD face in school are exacerbated when they also suffer from learning disabilities.

to concentrate. Researchers are uncertain why so many people with ADD also suffer from learning disabilities, but they speculate that since attention deficit disorder affects all areas of awareness, it magnifies the severity of any learning disability.

Another difficulty students with ADD face is due to their problems with organization. Although many people have messy work areas, the work areas of ADD sufferers are often in complete disarray. According to ADD expert Thom Hartmann, "Something usually separates messy ADD folks from their non-ADD counterparts. Non-ADD people can usually find what they need in their messes, while ADD people typically can't find anything."[40] Since they tend to lose things, it is hard for ADD students to move from class to class. They may misplace a book or assignment during any period of transition.

Because of their disorganization, students with attention deficit disorder have trouble doing any type of assignment that requires completing a series of tasks in sequence. Often other students do not want to work with ADD students on group assignments because they cannot be counted on to finish a task. Likewise, a lack of understanding by teachers often makes the problem worse. Students with ADD are repeatedly told that they need to be more serious about school, even though they are often struggling to succeed.

Similar problems follow ADD sufferers into the workplace, where the disorder's symptoms prevent many of them from ever reaching their full potential. ADD expert Edward M. Hallowell describes one of his ADD patients this way: "He leaves meetings abruptly, without warning, fails to return telephone calls, makes no attempt to hide it when he's bored, changes the subject almost in mid-sentence. 'He's brilliant,' an associate says, 'but he's so unpredictable.' "[41]

Symptoms of distractibility are often worsened by the design of many modern offices, where sound travels freely. According to ADD expert Dr. Kathleen G. Nadeau, "External distractions are

People with ADD often have difficulty holding a job because they are frequently disorganized and easily distracted in the workplace.

rampant in the current open office environment, which is very ADD-unfriendly."[42]

In addition to problems in the work environment itself, or perhaps because of these problems, people with ADD have trouble holding a job. Research shows that ADD sufferers change jobs more frequently than their peers, perhaps because their impulsiveness often causes them to chronically jump from job to job. Such job-hopping can result in failure to gain the promotions and pay raises that longer-term employees may enjoy.

There are other fiscal problems that people with ADD face. They often misplace or forget to pay bills, lose checkbooks and bank statements, and fail to keep accurate records of money spent. This can lead to chronically overdrawn accounts, late payment fees, and bad credit. As one ADD sufferer explains, "I kept forgetting to pay this bill and now they are charging me a huge late charge. I meant to pay it. I have plenty of money. I started paying it a half dozen times and got involved doing something else. I just have so many other things on my mind."[43]

Thrill-Seeking Behavior

Although their tendency to be disorganized can be costly to those with ADD, other aspects of their disorder can have even worse consequences. Impulsiveness leads many people with the disorder to develop risky, thrill-seeking behavior that often takes the form of compulsive shopping or an addiction to gambling. Research shows, for example, that at least 15 percent of those with ADD have a problem with gambling. Both compulsive shopping and gambling are addictive behaviors that can cripple ADD sufferers financially and ruin personal relationships. In general, people with the disorder have a greater rate of all addictive behaviors, including drug and alcohol abuse, than people without the disorder do.

Among the drugs that might be abused, marijuana is especially dangerous. ADD symptoms are more pronounced under the influence of marijuana, and research indicates it is more psychologically addictive among ADD sufferers than among others. Researchers believe that there may be a biological connection be-

ADD sufferers are at greater risk of abusing drugs and of engaging in other high-risk behaviors.

tween attention deficit disorder and addiction, which, they speculate, is connected to the deficiency of dopamine.

The tendency to take risks, which leads people with ADD to experiment with drugs, affects other aspects of their lives as well. For example, they also often exhibit high-risk behavior when they are driving. Research has shown that drivers with attention deficit disorder are more likely to speed and get into car accidents than other drivers. ADD sufferers seem to thrive on speed and will often drive recklessly, purposely exceeding speed limits and running traffic lights and stop signs. As one person with the disorder explains, "I drive fast. I race motorcycles. I've always walked the line. I wrecked seventeen cars by the time I was twenty-one. I had thirteen operations by the time I was twenty-five. Go fast; kind of walk that line. I don't do anything half speed, ever."[44] This behavior is often worsened because ADD sufferers frequently have trouble watching traffic and road signs simultaneously.

Because people with ADD tend to be emotionally intense, their thrill-seeking behavior sometimes takes the form of aggressive behavior. This is especially true among adolescents with ADD, who seem to be drawn to trouble. Even more than other teens, they tend to challenge authority and create conflict. Due to poor impulse control, these ADD sufferers often act dangerously without regard to the consequences of their actions.

Those consequences can, and often do, include jail. Studies have found that nearly 40 percent of male felons in medium-security prisons display the symptoms of ADD. When researchers classified prisoners by the type of crime they committed—either violent or nonviolent impulsive crimes—the percentage of nonviolent impulsive criminals who exhibited the symptoms of ADD was even greater than 40 percent. According to Hartmann, "Several psychiatrists suggest that, in their experience, the American prison popu-

Studies have shown that approximately 40 percent of America's prisoners display the symptoms of ADD, and some researchers believe that the correct number may be as high as 90 percent.

lation may be up to ninety percent ADD."[45] One study showed that many prisoners have a history of being treated for ADD as children but had ceased treatment for at least two years before committing a crime. Psychologists believe these ADD sufferers may have become involved in petty crimes in order to overcome the boredom that those with attention deficit disorder often feel.

In addition to boredom, people with the disorder often have sudden attacks of anger in which they lash out for no apparent reason at those close to them. These anger attacks are usually expressed as verbal assaults, but they can also take the form of physical assaults, especially among children with ADD, who are often involved in playground fights. The typical reaction of most adults to this behavior is to punish the aggressive child. However, according to ADD expert Gregg Soleil, "Punishing a child for something they can not easily control will cause confusion, and reinforce their sense of inadequacy, failure and low self-esteem—all counter productive."[46]

Family Problems

The problems with anger management and thrill-seeking behavior often have a negative impact not just on those with ADD but also on their families. ADD sufferers' need for excitement often motivates them to start arguments with family members. In addition, difficulties with inattention cause them to neglect chores and errands, making family members feel neglected. ADD expert Dr. Larry B. Silver describes a typical incident in an ADD sufferer's life:

> She went into the kitchen to start dinner. As she walked in, she saw some papers on the kitchen table and decided to sit down and go over them. As she was working on the papers, she looked up and noticed a note attached to her phone and remembered that she needed to make a phone call. As she was on the phone, she looked across and saw something on the counter. When she got off the phone, she went to the counter. At this point her children came in and asked when dinner would be ready. She had forgotten it entirely.[47]

The problems with inattentiveness are worsened because they are often mistaken for selfishness. People whose spouses have ADD frequently complain that their mates are self-centered and uncaring, showing no interest in their partners' needs. The spouse of one ADD sufferer explains: "I am so fed up with his endlessly forgetting things, not picking things up, interrupting, talking about himself, not being there in conversations, only remembering what concerns him, never what concerns me. I can not believe that ADD could make a person so selfish."[48] Researchers believe that this problem is one of the main reasons the divorce rate is higher among people with ADD than it is for the general population.

People with ADD often have difficulty with interpersonal relationships, and have a higher-than-average divorce rate.

Divorce is not the only problem that often affects the families of those with ADD. ADD teenagers' impulsiveness, inattention, and restlessness often are mistaken for rebelliousness by their families, leading to recurrent conflict in the home. Parents of ADD teens often feel frustrated by their offspring's behaviors. The parents set limits and rules, which are rarely followed. According to ADD experts Hallowell and Ratey, "This leads to chronic limit-setting by parents, with increasingly stringent penalties and tighter limitations. This, in turn, makes the child more defiant, less cooperative, and more alienated."[49]

The homes of teenagers with ADD often become battlegrounds. Yet even when parents are understanding and patient, the ADD teen suffers from a swirl of emotion, often including guilt. As one ADD sufferer recalls,

> For me, the worst thing about having ADD was how guilty I felt. I couldn't stay out of trouble, no matter how hard I tried. My parents would come home from work totally exhausted and ask me if I heated up dinner or picked up my brother or did whatever it was any normal kid did. Once I even left my little brother standing in front of school after dark. No matter how badly I screwed up, my parents always forgave me. I felt like a worthless freeloader who didn't deserve my parents' love.[50]

A Particular Burden for Women

Among women with ADD, studies indicate that problems at home are particularly pronounced. One recent study looked at the gender differences in cognitive abilities between males and females with the disorder. There were no gender differences in the test results, but female subjects, when asked to rate themselves regarding these same abilities, ranked themselves significantly lower than males did. Female subjects also exhibited far less self-confidence and greater feelings of anxiety, stress, and depression than the males did. Adding to this problem, studies have shown that the monthly hormonal changes women experience frequently worsen ADD symptoms, causing extreme irritability, rapid mood swings, and hypersensitivity, and leading to emotional overreactions.

These problems spill over into family life when women with ADD who are wives, mothers, and/or full-time workers begin to feel their lives are out of control. These women, like their non-ADD counterparts, expect to manage their own lives, families, and homes, and to succeed at their jobs. ADD symptoms make meeting these expectations extremely difficult, however. According to *ADDvance Magazine*, a magazine for and about women with ADD, "The job of homemaker is one of the most ADD-unfriendly jobs around. Homemaking requires women to function without external structure, juggling multiple, shifting responsibilities, to function despite frequent and often unavoidable interruptions, and to remain focused in a highly distracting environment."[51] Problems juggling these multiple roles cause some women with ADD to develop an eating disorder, which, experts believe, gives them a feeling of control over one aspect of their lives.

Associated Disorders

Some ADD sufferers develop other associated mental disorders that psychologists believe are often a direct result of the impact that attention deficit disorder has on their lives. Among these are anxiety disorder and depression. Although it is normal for people with ADD to suffer from anxiety due to the typical problems the disorder

Females with ADD seem to experience greater problems with self-esteem, anxiety, stress, and depression than their male counterparts.

causes in their lives, some of them develop a condition known as chronic irrational anxiety. According to Hallowell and Ratey,

> This is anxiety that the individual seeks out. The person often starts the day by rapidly scanning his or her mental horizon in search of something to worry about. Once a subject of worry has been located, the individual locks on it like a heat-sensing rocket and doesn't let go. No matter how trivial the subject or how painful the worry, the individual keeps the worry alive.[52]

Interestingly, experts believe that some ADD sufferers use this irrational worrying as a way to organize their otherwise confused thinking.

Similarly, the frustrations and failure that people with ADD experience often lead them to develop depression. However, because studies have shown that certain medications used to treat depression also seem to work well in treating ADD, experts believe that the two disorders share some kind of biochemical link. What this link is and whether it actually exists is still unknown. Whatever the nature of the link, some observers believe it is a potentially deadly one. A teacher of ADD students explains: "Every time I've come across a suicidal adolescent, it's been a very bright child with ADD. They can't handle that they're brilliant, yet unable to do their schoolwork. And the distortions of time-sense with ADD causes their lows to seem so painfully low that they get suicidal."[53]

Even when the symptoms of ADD do not cause someone to develop other disorders, the effects of attention deficit disorder permeate every aspect of a person's life. "I hate being like this," a person with ADD explains. "ADD has affected my whole life. But I'm not ashamed of who I am. I'm not a bad guy. I just can't stay focused. It's tough. People don't understand. But I've learned to live with it, and I'm doing pretty well, really I am."[54]

In the face of numerous difficulties, many with ADD have developed strategies for facing the problems caused by the disorder, allowing them to live fuller and happier lives.

Chapter 5

Living with ADD

M OST PEOPLE WITH ADD are able to meet the challenges posed by their condition by accepting attention deficit disorder as a part of their lives and developing strategies that help them to deal with it. According to ADD counselor Wilma Fellman, "Challenges can be the start or end of our 'whole picture.' We have the choice to live our lives 'leading with our strengths,' or offering our challenges as excuses for our failures."[55]

Successful people with ADD realize that although the disorder may be an explanation for a particular behavior, it is not an excuse for that behavior. These people understand how the symptoms of ADD affect them and are able to gain power over the disorder. This

understanding can help them prevent problems before they actually happen. For example, people with attention deficit disorder who are aware that their impulsiveness causes a problem with fast driving can consciously examine this behavior and deliberately drive more slowly. The person with ADD who does this takes responsibility for actions rather than blaming them on ADD.

Many ADD sufferers, like this university student, are determined to succeed despite the obstacles presented by their disability.

ADD sufferers can also gain power over the disorder by appreciating the positive traits—such as high energy, enthusiasm, creativity, spontaneity, boldness, and intuitiveness—that are common to many with ADD. They can use these traits to help develop individual responses to the roadblocks that ADD's symptoms may put in their paths. According to expert Ronald E. Jones, "The long term success of an ADD individual is enhanced by acquiring effective socially acceptable coping skills. Successful coping skills are those which build on a person's strengths."[56]

Coping with Inattentiveness

Developing coping skills to deal with inattention is often one of the greatest challenges to people with attention deficit disorder. They are bombarded by internal and external distractions, and coping with these distractions can be especially troublesome. As one ADD sufferer explains, "My mind is always wandering. I can't stay focused on one thing for long. My mind just goes, goes, goes."[57]

To help bring their attention back from its wanderings, experts suggest that they set a beeper to go off regularly. The idea is to return their focus to whatever task they need to accomplish. "I'll look up," one person with ADD explains, "and realize I was supposed to be somewhere at a certain time. If I had a beeper, it would help a lot."[58] Experts also suggest that ADD sufferers wear specially designed wristwatches with timers that act as both a training tool and as a reminder, helping the wearers to monitor their attentiveness.

Some people with ADD have been successful using meditation techniques, which help them to develop awareness of when the mind is wandering and to increase their attention span. ADD expert Thom Hartmann explains that among those with ADD, although "meditation was difficult at first, it became an important component of their lives once they made a habit of it."[59]

Many people with the disorder find that daily exercise helps focus their attention. Since physical activity increases blood flow to the brain, some experts believe that exercise improves the ability to focus by stimulating the release of neurotransmitters. One person with ADD reports, "If I don't run at least four times a week, I can't focus my attention."[60]

Some with ADD find that combining a physical activity with a mental one helps to keep them focused. For example, they may plan a business meeting while they are exercising, watch a movie while they are folding laundry, or pace the room while solving some kind of problem at home. Experts believe that for some people with attention deficit disorder, combining physical and mental activity may lessen internal distractions. This may account for the fact that students with ADD often are most successful in high-stimulation, hands-on, project-based classrooms where students do experiments and take field trips and where the emphasis is on doing rather than on sitting and listening.

Children at a summer camp for ADD sufferers participate in confidence-building team exercises. Many with ADD find that they are better able to focus when combining physical and mental activity.

Turning a Liability into an Asset

Some people with ADD turn their liabilities into assets. For instance, some find that although being distracted can be a problem, it can also be an asset since it enables them to work on a number of tasks simultaneously. In fact, some actually find that they need to do several things at the same time in order to accomplish anything. "I can do five or six things at once," explains a highly successful person with ADD. "I can read and listen to my mother at the same time. She makes me stop reading because she thinks I can't hear her. But I actually hear her better when I'm doing something else."[61]

Unfortunately, sometimes those who do not have ADD may misunderstand this type of behavior. As one person with ADD explains, "You're spilling over all the time. You're drumming your fingers, tapping your feet, humming a song, whistling, looking here, looking there, scratching, stretching, doodling, and people think you're not paying attention, but all you're doing is spilling over so you can pay attention."[62]

Creating an Appropriate Environment

Using background noise, another effective tool that assists in coping with internal and external distractions, is also frequently misunderstood by those who have not experienced ADD. Research has shown that many who have ADD can block out internal distractions and concentrate more easily if they have some sort of music or white noise playing in the background. According to experts,

> Sound screens are important. That's why having the TV or radio on in the background may be advantageous. At first it may seem like a distraction, but in reality, if the TV or music forms a "white noise" with an even level of intensity, it actually covers up discrepant noises that can be a distraction. The hum of a ceiling fan can do wonders to soothe and focus you.[63]

A sound screen is particularly effective for students with ADD to use while studying and for workers with ADD to use in the office.

It is essential that people with attention deficit disorder use individual strategies to create an environment which allows them to cope with internal and external distractions—no matter how that environment is perceived by others. This is why it is important that persons with ADD educate those close to them about the disorder rather than try to hide it. With just a little educating, friends can be an excellent support and help ADD sufferers with coping strategies. As one student with ADD explains, "My best friend reminds me every morning when it is time to take my medicine, and she walks me to the nurse's office. We share the same locker. She helps me keep track of my stuff."[64] At work or at school, when a boss or a teacher understands that a student or a worker has ADD, they can make accommodations that may help improve working and studying conditions. In fact, federal laws mandate that such accommodation be made.

How the Law Can Help

Under the federal law known as the Individuals with Disabilities Education Act (IDEA), all students have the right to receive an education that meets their individual educational needs. Moreover, many students with attention deficit disorder are considered to have a disability, and specific laws require that these students receive accommodations and modifications in their education, free of charge, so that they receive an education equal to that offered to nondisabled students. Similarly, many workers with ADD are also considered disabled, and the Americans with Disabilities Act (ADA) requires that accommodations be made in the workplace to meet their needs. A third law, the National Rehabilitation Act (NRA) section 504, also provides some added protection to people with disabilities, including attention deficit disorder.

IDEA guarantees an appropriate and free public education to children ages three through twenty-one who are disabled, and many students with ADD are covered by its provisions. Perhaps most importantly, the school, the student, and the student's parents are involved in developing an individualized education plan for the student. This program takes into account the indi-

A young boy with ADD (right) works with a classmate in a special-education class.

vidual's strengths and weaknesses and focuses on how to give the student an equal education, keeping in mind his or her unique needs. Some students are placed in small special-education classes where they work in smaller groups and receive individualized attention. Many students remain in their regular classes, but accommodations and modifications are made to help them reach their full potential. Some of these accommodations may include preferential seating in a less-distracting arrangement. One parent noted that such an accommodation greatly aided his son in coping with inattention. "The teacher knew he talked out of turn and was easily distracted, so she sat him up front next to her and that really helped him."[65] Other possible accommodations that can help students with ADD cope with forgetfulness and disorganization include shorter assignments, more time to complete tasks, modified tests, textbooks on tape, and dual sets of textbooks—one set to keep at school and another to keep at home.

The ADA and NRA section 504 cover disabled workers and students, including those with ADD, prohibiting discrimination against them and requiring that they be provided with reasonable accommodations to help them succeed. In all cases, the accommodations are made on an individual basis. It is up to individuals with ADD to understand their particular condition well enough to know what accommodations are needed. But even with the help of the law and the accommodations it provides, those with ADD still must develop and use specific coping skills to help them flourish.

Coping with Forgetfulness and Disorganization

Besides developing strategies to deal with inattention, individuals with ADD must cope with the problems of forgetfulness and disorganization that accompany their condition. Many with ADD keep lists and notes to remind themselves of what they have to do. One ADD sufferer explains, "Organization, that's the worst. I have to put notes on the front door that I can't miss before I go out so I don't forget anything. When I cook, I write myself a note to make sure I remember I have something in the oven or I'd burn down the place."[66]

Many of the tools used by those with ADD to help with organization are identical to those used by people who do not suffer from attention deficit disorder. However, individuals with ADD often need help in learning to use these tools. As one person with ADD recalls, "Someone once gave me one of those appointment books with all the compartments and sections to help me get organized. Just opening it up made me crazy. Instead of helping me, it completely intimidated me."[67] These tools, however, can be very effective when combined with strategies developed especially for people with ADD.

One such strategy is pattern planning, which helps those dealing with the disorder to organize their lives. Pattern planning means using a calendar or daily planner to manage time, which at first sounds like what many people who do not have ADD do. However, pattern planning, according to ADD experts, "is a system of time management that operates on the same system as automatic withdrawals from your bank account: by making the withdrawals (of money or time) automatic you don't have to plan them every time they happen."[68] ADD sufferers are instructed to record regular appointments into the pattern of their week to reduce problems with forgetfulness and to help them do these activities automatically. This may be as simple as a reminder to pick up a child from school everyday at 3:00 P.M., something a person who does not have ADD would probably not need to record.

Another special strategy is known as "chunking." Under this strategy, a person with ADD uses calendars and daily planners to help break up large assignments into several smaller tasks. Research shows that dividing large tasks into smaller ones is a particularly effective coping tool for those with ADD.

Making Career Choices

Like many other people, many who have ADD cope with problems with restlessness by playing on sports teams and exercising regularly. In addition many people with ADD try to harness their restlessness and high energy levels as an asset in their careers. As one man with ADD explains, "Going fast, fast, fast helped me at work. I was a contractor. I had so much energy. I worked outside in heat and cold, and I didn't tire. I'd work ten to twelve hours a day and recovered quickly. It was a great job for me. I couldn't sit behind a desk."[69]

Similarly, the thrill-seeking behavior typical of many with ADD can be harnessed in high-risk fields such as fire fighting and police work. There are people with ADD who work in emergency medicine, and they similarly thrive on the pace and excitement of a hospital emergency room. Willingness to take risks also helps ADD sufferers who own their own businesses. Research shows that a large number of people with ADD are business owners. In fact, in a recent study, a random group of business owners were tested for symptoms of ADD and about half were found to have the disorder. Many business owners with attention deficit disorder are highly successful, especially when they hire other people to handle routine paperwork and financial details.

People with ADD are often drawn to high-risk, exciting careers such as police work, where high energy and restlessness can be an asset.

Harnessing Creativity

Research has also shown that people with ADD score higher on tests of creativity than the general population. Experts believe that the impulsiveness displayed by those with ADD allows them to take creative risks. That impulsiveness, combined with their lack of inhibition, makes these people unafraid to try the new and what others might consider outrageous, often leading to the development of new solutions to old problems. In addition, experts also believe that inattention, which often leads to daydreaming, can be the first step in such creative undertakings as writing and painting. As one artist with ADD explains, "I guess ADD helps with creativity because I'm a good artist. It makes me work harder. I push people on to the extreme. I push myself to the extreme too."[70]

Wandering attention also allows people with attention deficit disorder to view a problem from a variety of angles, possibly seeing answers that more focused people might miss. According to one highly creative person with ADD, "The trait of constantly shifting point of view is a fabulous asset here. It's what lets you see unexpected things where others see only the obvious. It's like looking for an elusive piece of a jigsaw puzzle, picking something up, and discovering you don't have what you sought, but you found something even better."[71]

Hyperfocus

An ADD person's ability to hyperfocus is also important to the creative process. Hyperfocus often occurs when people with ADD are performing a pleasurable task. While hyperfocusing, they will become so intensely focused and engrossed in the activity that they will become completely unaware of time, place, and any activity around them. "It's like tunnel vision," says one young woman about her experience while hyperfocusing. "I'll start working on a painting and won't stop until I'm done. While I'm working, my family will be talking to me and I won't even hear them. But later I'll answer questions to a conversation that they had five hours ago."[72]

The creative energy displayed by many who have been diagnosed with ADD tempts many people to speculate whether many highly creative people in history were in fact affected by ADD. Such speculation is, of course, pointless. For most people with ADD, the issue is not whether a Renaissance artist or famous novelist shared their disorder, but what the future might hold in the way of better treatments or a cure.

Chapter 6

What the Future Holds

PEOPLE WITH ADD face many challenges and know that there is no definitive known cause, diagnosis, or treatment for their condition. But research on attention deficit disorder is ongoing, and many of these studies have proven productive. Experts believe that research will lead to a better understanding of what causes the disorder and to more accurate diagnosis and treatment.

Using Brain Imaging

Researchers are beginning to find new data on the involvement of the brain in attention deficit disorder. Using techniques such as magnetic resonance imaging (MRI), doctors can produce cross-sections of tissue without ever touching the patient's brain. Researchers are using MRI to investigate how differences between the right and left sides of the brain may be involved in ADD. Studies of possible developmental changes in specific parts of the brain are also being done using MRI technology. One such study by the National Institute of Mental Health used magnetic resonance imaging to measure and compare the brains of boys with ADD to those of boys without the disorder. The study found that the right side of the anterior frontal lobes of the boys with ADD was about 5 percent smaller than that of their peers. It also found that the right caudate, the section of the brain involved in impulse control, was also smaller. Other studies tend to confirm that some kind of relationship exists between the size of these structures and ADD, but a direct causal link has yet to be proved.

Another imaging technique, positron emission tomography (PET), is being used to compare the brain activity in men with ADD to that in men without the disorder. The researchers found that the men with ADD had much higher levels of blood flow in their brains than their non-ADD peers when tasks involving thinking were being performed, and lower blood flow the rest of the time. This study has led experts to question whether the level of blood flow to the brain is somehow involved in inhibiting attentiveness.

Other brain imaging techniques are also being used to measure specific brain functions and to determine what part these functions may play in ADD. Single photon emission computed tomography (SPECT) is one such tool. A recent study using the diagnostic radioactive tracer Altropane to perform SPECT showed a far greater-than-normal number of dopamine neurotransmitters in the brains of all of the subjects tested. This is the first study to show that there is a measurable chemical difference in the brains of people with ADD. According to nuclear medicine expert Dr. Alan Fischman, "The findings in this study are very significant, and demonstrate that Altropane potentially could be

PET scans of a brain made while the patient was performing cognitive tasks. Researchers are able to use such technology to compare brain activity of ADD and non-ADD subjects.

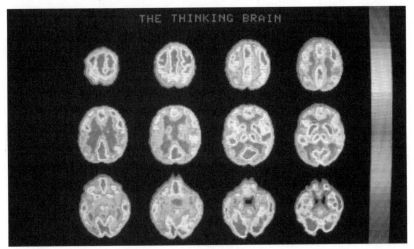

of great value in establishing the existence of an objective biological abnormality in ADHD."[73] Further studies are being done using Altropane-SPECT brain scans to prove conclusively that people with ADD have an excessive amount of dopamine in their brains.

Improving Diagnosis

Altropane-SPECT brain imagery research is not only important in helping to discover a biochemical cause of ADD, but it is also essential to the development of a definitive and accurate tool for diagnosing the disorder. This is especially important in light of the controversy and questions involved with the current forms of diagnosis. Many experts believe that using behavioral criteria such as those defined in the American Psychiatric Association's *Diagnostic and Statistical Manual* is too subjective, with the result that many cases of ADD have been misdiagnosed or have gone undiagnosed while other problems have been wrongly labeled as ADD. If proved effective, using Altropane-SPECT brain scans would provide an objective diagnostic tool for ADD. Dr. Edward

SPECT brain imaging (pictured), which is used to study the chemical differences in the brains of ADD sufferers, may someday provide an objective diagnostic tool for ADD.

M. Hallowell believes that Altropane-SPECT brain imaging is "the most promising development seen in a long time in terms of our coming up with an actual physical test that could help us pin down the diagnosis of ADHD."[74]

Other Studies into the Causes of ADD

In addition to brain studies, many researchers are examining other organs in hopes of finding a link to the disorder. One study, for example, examined the relationship of the thyroid gland to ADD in children. The subjects were all children diagnosed as having ADD, and all were found to have higher-than-normal thyroid hormone production. They were treated with a drug called Neomercazole, which is commonly used to reduce the production of thyroid hormones. After treatment with the drug, the subjects' attention spans increased, and they were much less restless and hyperactive. This study has led researchers to speculate about a connection between ADD and hyperthyroidism, and further studies are being undertaken in this area.

Other recent studies looked at a number of birth factors and their possible links to ADD. One study investigated a possible link between women who smoked during pregnancy and ADD. This study found that women who smoked during pregnancy were two times more likely than their nonsmoking peers to have children who have attention deficit disorder. Although this study did not find a conclusive link between smoking and ADD, it does provide an additional reason why expectant mothers should avoid tobacco smoke. Additional ongoing studies are investigating whether illnesses or injuries to expectant mothers could cause biochemical changes in their fetus' brains, resulting in ADD. Other studies are examining whether long labor, having a baby at a young age, or low birth weight (often caused by substance abuse) may lead to the development of attention deficit disorder. These studies are still inconclusive, however.

Other ongoing studies are examining the possible connection between diet and the symptoms of ADD. One such study compared metabolism of fatty acids such as omega-3 by children with ADD to the metabolism of these substances by children without the disorder. Researchers found that the children with ADD had considerably lower levels of key fatty acids in their bloodstream. Researchers are unsure why this was so. What researchers found most compelling are the similarities between the symptoms of essential fatty acid deficiency and the symptoms of ADD. Symptoms of such a deficiency include behavioral problems, memory loss, frequent temper tantrums, sleep disorders, depression, hyperactivity, and learning problems. Experts theorize that certain fatty acids are needed to maintain and build neurotransmitters. Researchers are unsure about the relationship between deficiencies in essential fatty acids and ADD, but some patients with ADD are adding omega-3 to their diets in hopes of relieving ADD symptoms.

Other studies, still in their beginning stages, are investigating the role of genetics in causing ADD. Scientists believe that there are several specific genes for ADD, and they are attempting to identify and isolate them.

The relationship between sleep disorders and ADD is also being studied. Recent studies investigating deep dream states indi-

A scientist studies human DNA patterns. Researchers are currently trying to identify and isolate the specific genes that might cause ADD.

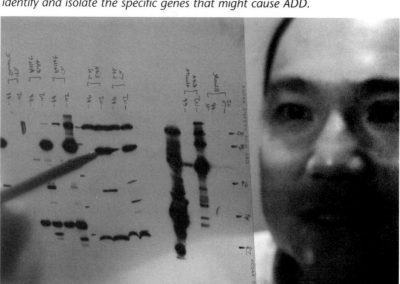

cate that such a state is essential for learning to become a part of one's memory. Researchers believe that ADD sufferers' sleep problems interfere with their deep dream state, causing their learning problems.

Future Pharmaceutical Treatment

In addition to research into the causes of ADD, many studies are being conducted in the hopes of developing new and better medication for treating attention deficit disorder. One such study investigated a new class of drugs specifically aimed at helping adults with ADD who have not responded positively to treatment with psychostimulants. The drug, designated as ABT 418, was especially effective in relieving problems of inattention in the subjects with the least severe cases of ADD. More encouraging still, this drug had very few side effects. Studies are continuing on this medication and others like it.

Another promising medication, designated as GT2331, is used to enhance cognitive abilities in patients. In clinical trials, subjects were found to have higher levels of alertness and lower levels of inattention than they had without the medication. Researchers found the results encouraging and are now focusing on finding an effective and safe dosage level of this drug.

Researchers continue to search for new medications, such as the psychostimulant Adderall, which is already on the market and which they hope is longer lasting than Ritalin. Adderal, its advocates say, would be helpful to people with ADD who currently must take multiple doses of Ritalin. Other research is focusing on the effect of the antidepressant medication Prozac on subjects with attention deficit disorder. The results are promising. Subjects given the medication exhibit diminished symptoms of restlessness, and further studies are being undertaken.

Future Nonpharmaceutical Treatment

Although some who have ADD get relief using biofeedback, one study combined biofeedback techniques with hypnosis. One group of subjects used biofeedback training to improve attentiveness, focus, and the ability to learn. A second group of subjects used the same biofeedback techniques but were also hypnotized during the process. Researchers told subjects under hypnosis that "in this special state of alertness you will be able to focus your attention any way you like, you can concentrate as completely as you desire."[75] Both groups showed long-lasting improvement. However, the group that was hypnotized improved much more quickly. Research on the use of biofeedback alone and combined with other techniques is ongoing.

Long-Term Follow-Up

Studies are also underway to determine what childhood ADD treatments are most effective in helping children with the disorder deal with ADD effectively later in life. Other studies are investigating the long-term effect of attention deficit disorder on families. Children with ADD are being followed into adulthood. How well or poorly they are functioning in comparison to their non-ADD brothers or sisters is being examined. In addition, how these subjects deal with their own children is also being studied.

Researchers continue to study the effectiveness of biofeedback, an alternative therapy that has been shown to help ADD sufferers focus their attention.

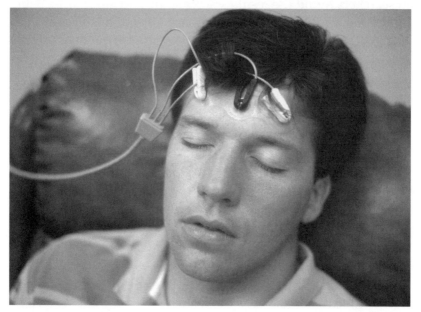

A nine-year-old with ADD poses with his sister. Long-term studies are currently underway that follow children with ADD into adulthood to see how well they are functioning in comparison to their non-ADD siblings.

Although attention deficit disorder in many ways remains an enigma, scientists continue working to solve its mysteries. Those who suffer from ADD can realistically hope that eventually the confusion and misunderstanding that surround the disorder will be alleviated. Perhaps in the not so distant future researchers will discover a cure, and attention deficit disorder will become only a memory.

Notes

Introduction: A Neurological Syndrome
1. Josh, interview by author, Dallas, August 9, 2000.
2. Edward M. Hallowell and John J. Ratey, *Answers to Distraction.* New York: Pantheon Books, 1994, p. 3.

Chapter 1: A Misunderstood Problem
3. Robert T. Taucher, *Cultures of Healing.* New York: W. H. Freeman, 1995, p. 58.
4. Quoted in Edward M. Hallowell and John J. Ratey, *Driven to Distraction.* New York: Touchstone Books, 1994, p. 272.
5. Quoted in Hallowell and Ratey, *Driven to Distraction,* p. 271.
6. Quoted in Lawrence H. Diller, *Running on Ritalin.* New York: Bantam Books, 1998, p. 148.
7. Thom Hartmann, *Attention Deficit Disorder: A Different Perception.* Lancaster, PA: Underwood-Miller, 1993, p. xxi.

Chapter 2: Causes and Diagnosis
8. Hallowell and Ratey, *Driven to Distraction,* p. 42.
9. Pamela, interview by author, Dallas, August 15, 2000.
10. Diller, *Running on Ritalin,* p. 65.
11. Larry B. Silver, *The Misunderstood Child: A Guide for Parents of Children with Learning Disabilities.* New York: Times Books, 1998, p. 208.
12. Quoted in Bonnie Cramond, "The Coincidence of Attention Deficit Hyperactivity Disorder and Creativity," Born to Explore. www.borntoexplore.org/adhd.htm.
13. Quoted in Steven M. Nordby, "Problems in Identification and Assessment of ADHD," October 1994. http://members.aol.com/svennord/ed/adhd.htm.
14. Hallowell and Ratey, *Driven to Distraction,* p. 196.
15. Diller, *Running on Ritalin,* p. 61.
16. Hallowell and Ratey, *Driven to Distraction,* p. 216.

Chapter 3: Treatment
17. Hallowell and Ratey, *Driven to Distraction,* p. 216.

18. Hallowell and Ratey, *Driven to Distraction*, p. 246.

19. Al, interview by author, New York, August 13, 2000.

20. Hallowell and Ratey, *Driven to Distraction*, p. 222.

21. Quoted in Lisa Horan, "AD/HD Coaching: Empowering People to Succeed," *Idea*, Summer 1999. www.chadd.org/attention/attnv6n1p12.htm.

22. Al, interview.

23. Hallowell and Ratey, *Driven to Distraction*, p. 236.

24. Michael, interview by author, Flowermound, Texas, August 13, 2000.

25. Julia, interview by author, Dallas, May 16, 2000.

26. Julia, interview.

27. Hartmann, *Attention Deficit Disorder*, p. 61.

28. Diller, *Running on Ritalin*, p. 264.

29. Jeanie Davis, "Ritalin—Prescriptions Don't Seem to Matter for Some: Speed-Like Drug Abused by Kids *and* Adults," WebMD Health, May 9, 2000. www.my.webmd.com/content/article/1728.57356.

30. Silver, *The Misunderstood Child*, p. 329.

Chapter 4: Problems with Few Solutions

31. Hallowell and Ratey, *Driven to Distraction*, p. 76.

32. Quoted in Hartmann, *Attention Deficit Disorder*, p. 71.

33. Ron, interview by author, Dallas, August 14, 2000.

34. Diller, *Running on Ritalin*, p. 132.

35. Quoted in Kevin R. Murphy and Suzanne Le Vert, *Out of the Fog*. New York: Skyline, 1995, p. 219.

36. Ron, interview.

37. Stephen W. Garber, Marianne Daniels Garber, and Robyn Freedman Spizman, *Beyond Ritalin*. New York: Villard, 1996, p. 137.

38. Ronnie, interview by author, Dallas, August 15, 2000.

39. Garber, Garber, and Spizman, *Beyond Ritalin*, p. 43.

40. Hartmann, *Attention Deficit Disorder*, p. 3.

41. Hallowell and Ratey, *Answers to Distraction*, p. 79.

42. Kathleen G. Nadeau, "Top Ten Traps in the Workplace," National Attention Deficit Disorder Association. www.add.org/content/work/traps.htm.

43. Ron, interview.
44. Ronnie, interview.
45. Hartmann, *Attention Deficit Disorder*, p. 6.
46. Gregg Soleil, "First Steps to Effective Intervention: A Policy Brief by Appalachia Educational Laboratory," ADD Net UK, 1995. www.btinternet.com/~black.ice/addnet/identify.html.
47. Silver, *The Misunderstood Child*, p. 216.
48. Quoted in Hallowell and Ratey, *Answers to Distraction*, p. 157.
49. Hallowell and Ratey, *Driven to Distraction*, p. 12.
50. Anonymous, interview by author, Dallas, June 27, 2000.
51. *ADDvance Magazine*, "ADD in the Workplace: Juggling the Dual Responsibility of Home and Work." www.addvance.com/article11.html.
52. Hallowell and Ratey, *Driven to Distraction*, p. 155.
53. Quoted in Hartmann, *Attention Deficit Disorder*, p. 106.
54. Ron, interview.

Chapter 5: Living with ADD

55. Wilma Fellman, "Career Challenges and ADD: We Have a Choice," National Attention Deficit Disorder Association. www.add.org/content/work/wilmal.htm4.
56. Ronald E. Jones, "The Transition of Children with ADD into Successful Adults." www.enteract.com/~peregrin/add/trans.txt.
57. Ron, interview.
58. Ronnie, interview.
59. Hartmann, *Attention Deficit Disorder*, p. 30.
60. Quoted in Hartmann, *Attention Deficit Disorder*, p. 33.
61. Julia, interview.
62. Quoted in Edward M. Hallowell, "What's It Like to Have ADD?" National Attention Deficit Disorder Association, 1992. www. add.org/context/abc/hallowell.htm.
63. Lynn Weiss, *Attention Deficit Hyperactivity Disorder and Learning Disabilities*. Dallas: Taylor, 1992, p. 87.
64. Julia, interview.
65. Al, interview.
66. Ron, interview.

67. Quoted in Murphy and Le Vert, *Out of the Fog*, p. 52.
68. Hallowell and Ratey, *Driven to Distraction*, p. 222.
69. Ronnie, interview.
70. Julia, interview.
71. Quoted in Hartmann, *Attention Deficit Disorder*, p. 59.
72. Julia, interview.

Chapter 6: What the Future Holds

73. Alan Fischman, "Brain Scan Shows ADHD," Adders Organization. www.adders.org/research.htm.
74. Quoted in Fischman, "Brain Scans Shows ADHD."
75. Quoted in Arreed Barabasz and Marianne Barabasz, "Attention Deficit Hyperactivity Disorder: Neurological Basis and Treatment Alternatives," *Journal of Neurotherapy*. www.snr-jnt.org/JournalNT/JNT(1-1)1.html.

Glossary

antidepressant: A drug used to fight depression.

anxiety disorder: A mental disorder that causes a person to be overly worried.

axon: A neuron that carries outgoing neurotransmitters.

behavioral therapies: Techniques used to change a person's behavior.

biofeedback: A process that teaches a person to control a specific body function.

bipolar disorder: A mental disorder characterized by periods of great happiness alternating with periods of deep depression.

cerebrum: The part of the brain where thought occurs.

clinical history: A patient's history of mental and physical growth.

cognitive behavioral therapy: A technique to change a person's learning behavior.

conduct disorder: A mental disorder that causes a person to exhibit extreme antisocial behavior.

depression: A mental disorder that causes feelings of great sadness.

developmental history: A patient's history of physical development.

dopamine: A neurotransmitter.

eating disorders: A group of mental disorders that cause a person to alter his or her intake of food.

essential fatty acids: Nutrients found in fatty fish, nuts, and olive oil.

hyperactive: To be overactive physically.

hyperfocus: A state of attentiveness in which all outside stimuli is blotted out by the mind.

hyperkinetic: To be overactive physically.

hyperthyroidism: A disorder caused by an overactive thyroid gland.

learning disability: A problem in learning that is not a result of poor intelligence or poor teaching.

magnetic resonance imaging (MRI): A technique using radio waves to produce images of the brain.

multimodal approach: An ADD treatment approach that uses a variety of techniques.

neurofeedback: A process through which a person uses specialized instruments to receive signals of changes in his or her body functions in order to change and control these functions.

neurological: Having to do with the brain and nervous system.

neurosis: A disorder of the mind or emotions.

neurotransmitter: A chemical that travels from cell to cell in the brain to either excite or inhibit action.

obsessive-compulsive disorder: A mental disorder that causes a person to perform repetitive behavior and have recurrent bothersome ideas.

oppositional defiant disorder: A mental disorder that causes a person to argue and openly defy those in authority.

phobias: Irrational fears.

placebo: An ineffective medication, such as a sugar pill, often used in research studies as a control.

positron emission tomography (PET): A medical procedure that uses radioactive tracers and computer technology to x-ray the brain.

psychiatrists: Medical doctors who treat mental illnesses.

psychoanalysis: A talk therapy technique developed by Freud to investigate and cure mental disorders.

psychologists: Specialists who deal with mental problems.

psychostimulant: A drug that causes the user to feel both mentally and physically alert and energetic.

schizophrenia: A mental disease that causes a person to withdraw from reality.

seasonal mood disorder: A mental disorder that is characterized by depression during the winter months.

self-esteem: Belief in oneself.

self-observation: An understanding of one's being and actions.

single photon emission computed tomography (SPECT): A medical procedure that uses radioactive tracers to form images of the circulation and volume of blood in the brain.

structuring: A treatment for ADD that involves helping the patient organize his or her life.

Tourette's syndrome: A mental disorder that affects behavior, and often results in uncontrollable facial tics.

trans-fatty acids: Man-made nutrients found in processed food and margarine.

visual-motor skills: Skills using eye-to-hand coordination.

Organizations to Contact

Adult ADD Association
1225 E. Sunset Dr., # 640
Bellingham, WA 98226
(360) 647-6681
e-mail: http://dfhw32@prodigy.com

This organization provides support and information on adult ADD. It also provides information on local support groups.

Children and Adults with Attention Deficit Disorder (CH.A.D.D.)
8181 Professional Pl., Suite 201
Landover, MD 20785
(800) 233-4050
fax: (301) 306-7090
website: www.chadd.org

CH.A.D.D. is a nonprofit international support group for people with ADD and their families. It supports research on ADD, lobbies for the rights of people with the disorder, and provides up-to-the-minute legislative information. It publishes *Attention*, a quarterly magazine featuring the work of ADD experts, and it holds an annual conference that deals with all ADD issues.

National Attention Deficit Disorder Association
1788 Second St., Suite 200
Highland Park, IL 60035
(847) 432-ADDA
fax: (847) 432-5874
e-mail: mail@add.org
website: www.add.org
This international nonprofit organization provides educational resources, information, and support to people with ADD and their families. It lobbies for the rights of ADD sufferers and supports training and research into the causes and treatments of

ADD. It publishes *Challenge,* a bimonthly newsletter that features articles by ADD experts. It also provides information on local support groups and local ADD professionals. It holds an annual conference on ADD issues featuring prominent experts.

National Coaching Network
Box 353
Lafayette Hill, PA 19444

The National Coaching Network provides information on ADD coaching and the names of professional ADD coaches to contact.

For Further Reading

Books

Jim Barmeier, *The Brain.* San Diego: Lucent Books, 1996. Explains how the brain works.

Kate Kelly and Peggy Ramundo, *You Mean I'm Not Lazy, Stupid, or Crazy?! A Self-Help Book for Adults with Attention Deficit Disorder.* New York: Fireside, 1996. Talks about the experiences of adults with ADD and discusses ways to cope with the disorder.

Kathleen G. Nadeau, *Help 4ADD@ School.* Bethesda, MD: Advantage Books, 1998. Offers practical tips for students with ADD about how to succeed in high school.

Judyth Reichenberg-Ullman and Robert Ullman, *Ritalin-Free Kids: Safe and Effective Homeopathic Medicine for ADD and Other Behavioral and Learning Problems.* Rocklin, CA: Prima, 1996. Looks at alternative treatments for ADD.

Sari Solden, *Women with Attention Deficit Disorder: Embracing Disorganization at Home and in the Workplace.* Penn Valley, CA: Underwood, 1995. Focuses on females with ADD and the special challenges they face.

James Lawrence Thomas, *Do You Have Attention Deficit Disorder?* New York: Dell, 1996. Provides facts on the symptoms, diagnosis, and treatment of ADD along with self-diagnostic quizzes and checklists.

Websites

ADHD News (www.adhdnews.com). This website offers a free subscription to an ADD newsletter, extensive legal information, on-line support groups, many ADD links, and e-mail discussion groups.

Child Development Institute (www.cdipage.com/adhd.htm). This website provides information about every aspect of ADD, including links to discussion groups.

Healthlink USA (www.healthlinkusa.com/35feat.htm). This

website gives ten pages of links to information on every aspect of ADD.

Mediconsult (www.mediconsult.com). Mediconsult provides information on recent medical research on the disorder.

National Library of Medicine (www.ncbi.nlm.nih.gov/entrez/query.fcgi). The latest research on ADD is provided on this site.

Northern County Psychiatric Associates (www.ncpamd.com). This site provides a large collection of articles on adult and pediatric ADD.

One A.D.D. Place (www.oneaddplace.com). This website provides numerous articles, resources, and links to all aspects of the disorder.

Robin's Nest (www.robinsnest.com/articles/adds.html). Robin's Nest offers multiple links dealing with every aspect of ADD, including how to succeed in school, medication charts, and assessment material.

Works Consulted

Books

American Psychiatric Association, *Diagnostic and Statistical Manual of Mental Disorders*. 4th ed. Washington, DC: American Psychiatric Association, 1994. Provides the criteria for the diagnosis of ADD.

Lawrence H. Diller, *Running on Ritalin*. New York: Bantam Books, 1998. Detailed work on the cause, diagnosis, and treatment of ADD, with a look at the controversy surrounding Ritalin use.

Stephen W. Garber, Marianne Daniels Garber, and Robyn Freedman Spizman, *Beyond Ritalin*. New York: Villard, 1996. A detailed examination of the cause, diagnosis, and treatment of ADD, including a close study of the possible negative effects of Ritalin.

Edward M. Hallowell and John J. Ratey, *Answers to Distraction*. New York: Pantheon Books, 1994. A comprehensive look at ADD that uses patients' own experiences as a springboard to a discussion on every aspect of the disorder.

————, *Driven to Distraction*. New York: Touchstone Books, 1994. Written in question-and-answer form, this book answers all sorts of questions from ADD patients in a straightforward, concise manner.

Thom Hartmann, *Attention Deficit Disorder: A Different Perception*. Lancaster, PA: Underwood-Miller, 1993. An interesting look at ADD as an adaptive style rather than as a disorder.

Harold S. Koplewicz, *It's Nobody's Fault*. New York: Random House, 1996. Explains the biological causes of ADD and offers advice on diagnosis and treatment.

Patricia H. Latham and Peter S. Latham, *Higher Education Services for Students with Attention Deficit Disorder and Learning Disabilities: A Legal Guide*. Washington, DC: NCLLD, 1994. A guide to the laws that protect students with ADD in college.

Harold N. Levinson, *Total Concentration*. New York: M. Evans,

1990. Strategies on how to develop better powers of concentration.

Kevin R. Murphy and Suzanne Le Vert, *Out of the Fog*. New York: Skyline, 1995. This book looks at ADD in adults.

Larry B. Silver, *The Misunderstood Child: A Guide for Parents of Children with Learning Disabilities*. New York: Times Books, 1998. Looks at different psychological disorders and disabilities and how they affect children.

Robert T. Taucher, *Cultures of Healing*. New York: W. H. Freeman, 1995. A historical look at mental illness.

Lynn Weiss, *Attention Deficit Hyperactivity Disorder and Learning Disabilities*. Dallas: Taylor, 1992. Discusses the effects of ADD on learning.

Internet Sources

ADDvance Magazine, "ADD in the Workplace: Juggling the Dual Responsibility of Home and Work." www.addvance.com/article 11.html.

Arreed Barabasz and Marianne Barabasz, "Attention Deficit Hyperactivity Disorder: Neurological Basis and Treatment Alternatives," *Journal of Neurotherapy.* www.snr-jnt.org/JournalNT/ JNT(1-1)1.html.

Bonnie Cramond, "The Coincidence of Attention Deficit Hyperactivity Disorder and Creativity," Born to Explore. www. borntoexplore.org/adhd.htm.

James J. Crist, "ADHD: A Teenager's Guide," National Attention Deficit Disorder Association. www.add.org/content/teens/ tguide.htm.

Jeanie Davis, "Ritalin—Prescriptions Don't Seem to Matter for Some: Speed-Like Drug Abused by Kids *and* Adults," WebMD Health, May 9, 2000. www.my.webmd.com/content/article/ 1728.57356.

Wilma Fellman, "Career Challenges and ADD: We Have a Choice," National Attention Deficit Disorder Association. www.add.org/content/work/wilmal.htm4.

Alan Fischman, "Brain Scan Shows ADHD," Adders Organization. www.adders.org/research.htm.

Teresa Gallagher, "Born to Explore: The Other Side of ADD," Born to Explore. www.borntoexplore.org/.

Edward M. Hallowell, "What's It Like to Have ADD?" National Attention Deficit Disorder Association, 1992. www.add.org/content/abc/hallowell.htm.

Lisa Horan, "AD/HD Coaching: Empowering People to Succeed," *Idea,* Summer 1999. www.chadd.org/attention/attnv6n1p12.htm.

Ronald E. Jones, "The Transition of Children with ADD into Successful Adults." www.enteract.com/~peregrin/add/trans.txt.

Patricia H. Latham, "Attention Deficit Disorder in College Faculty and Students: Partners in Education," National Attention Deficit Disorder Association. www.add.org/content/legal/college.htm.

Kathleen G. Nadeau, "Top Ten Traps in the Workplace," National Attention Deficit Disorder Association. www.add.org/content/work/traps.htm.

Steven M. Nordby, "Problems in Identification and Assessment of ADHD," October 1994. http://members.aol.com/svennord/ed/adhd.htm.

Harvey C. Parker, "Assessment of Attention Deficit Disorders: A Team Approach," One A.D.D. Place. www.oneaddplace.com/articles/adassess.htm.

Gregg Soleil, "First Steps to Effective Intervention: A Policy Brief by Appalachia Educational Laboratory," ADD Net UK, 1995. www.btinternet.com/~black.ice/addnet/identify.html.

Index

schools
  accommodations in, 61–64
  hands-on learning in, 60
  problems in, 31, 47–50
seasonal mood disorder, 24
secondary symptoms, 44–57
self-esteem, 30, 33, 44–45
selfishness, 53–54
sight problems, 24
Silver, Larry B., 24, 41, 53
single photon emission computed
  tomography (SPECT), 69–71
skullcap, 41
sleep patterns, 22
  deep dream state and, 72–73
  fatty acid deficiency and, 72
  medication and, 36–37
slow growth patterns, 37
social problems, 15, 44–57
social-skills training, 33
Soleil, Gregg, 53
Spizman, Robyn Freedman, 46–47
Still, George Frederick, 14–15
stimulants, 15–16
  for adults, 73
  decision to medicate and, 35–40
  see also specific stimulants
stomachaches, 38
stress, 55–56
  see also anxiety; depression
structuring, 32–33, 59
substance abuse, 38–40, 45, 50–51
sugar, 17–18
suicidal tendencies, 57
symptoms, 8–10
  checklist of, 25–26
  hyperactivity as, 13, 27, 38, 71
  inattentiveness as, 27–28, 53–54,
    67
  restlessness as, 13, 24, 28, 46
  *see also Diagnostic and Statistical
    Manual of Mental Disorders
    (DSM-IV)*

tactile learning, 60
talking, excessive, 28, 38
tasks
  "chunking," 65
  performing multiple, 61
teachers, 31, 49, 62
teenagers. *See* adolescents
tests, diagnostic, 22
therapy, 30–34
  see also treatment
thrill-seeking behavior, 39, 50–53,
  65
thyroid problems, 24, 71
tics, involuntary, 38
time management, 22, 32–33, 59
  see also organization skills
Tourette's syndrome, 38
trauma memory, 14
treatment
  alternative, 40–43, 73–74
  medication and, 29–30
  in the Middle Ages, 12
  multimodal, 30–35
  for neurasthenia, 13
  psychoanalysis and, 14, 16

University of Michigan, 40

valerian, 41
vision problems, 24

water therapy, 13
white noise, 61–62
workplace
  career choices and, 65
  environment of, 61–64
  problems in, 47–50
worrying. *See* anxiety
wristwatches, specially designed,
  59

X rays. *See* imaging techniques,
  brain

Picture Credits

About the Author

Barbara Sheen holds a master's degree in curriculum and instruction from Long Island University in New York. She has been a writer and educator for thirty years. Her writing has been published in the United States and Europe, and includes four books for young people, including two bilingual (English-Spanish) books, and one book in German. She has also published three books for adults. She currently lives in Texas with her husband and two cats.